JUDGE
FOR YOURSELVES

JUDGE
FOR YOURSELVES

READING
1 CORINTHIANS

ROBERT
EVANS

DARTON · LONGMAN + TODD

First published in 2003 by
Darton, Longman and Todd Ltd
1 Spencer Court
140–142 Wandsworth High Street
London SW18 4JJ

ISBN 0–232–52491–2

A catalogue record for this book is available from the British Library.

The Scripture quotations in this publication are taken from the New Revised
Standard Version © 1989, 1995. Division of Christian Education of the National
Council of the Churches of Christ in the United States of America.

Designed by Sandie Boccacci
Phototypeset by 11.75/13.25pt Perpetua
by Intype Libra Limited
Printed and bound in Great Britain by
Page Bros, Norwich, Norfolk

For Ruth, co-worker.

kai gar autē prostatis pollōn egenēthē
kai emou autou (Rom. 16:2)

Contents

Introduction

The title of this book echoes a phrase Paul uses twice to the Christians in Corinth about issues of belief and behaviour, and the aim of *Judge for Yourselves* is to help you as the reader to make your own judgements about what Paul has to say. In the spirit of this instruction, this book does not merely introduce Paul's message and method, but also inducts the reader into how to go about reading his letters, to consider the method and discover the message.

Paul has been immensely influential in the formation of the Church's theology, but is a contentious figure even among Christian readers of the New Testament. Indeed, it is difficult not to be controversial about Paul. There is a wealth of scholarly and popular books about Paul and the letters, some investigating the history and sociology of his congregations, some giving an account of his theology, some seeking to apply his theology to Christian thought and action today. This book uses this literature but in such a way as to help a reader to identify Paul's key theological ideas and to assess how he applies them to the situations of Christian lives.

Judge for Yourselves reveals Paul as an extraordinary 'applied' or practical theologian. He has overarching theological principles, based on proclaiming 'Christ crucified' which he can relate to the most mundane things – and relate mundane things to those principles. The letters are occasioned by and directed to real people and situations, and seeing how Paul applies his theology can lead readers to consider what it means to do the same: to apply the principles but to today's situations.

You will be encouraged to recognise your own reading perspective and those of other readers of these texts. Paul's theology has been so influential in the development of Christian belief and thought that it is hard not to import what may be later Christian doctrines and attitudes back into our reading of his letters. We may need to check out some of our assumptions and prejudgements against what the texts actually say. At the close of each chapter, you will be encouraged to reflect on the questions that have been posed, and to consider how far you are or are not persuaded by what Paul has written, or by how this author has read him.

In the first chapter, Paul's shortest letter, Philemon, is used as a case study in Pauline method and acts as an introduction to the approach pursued in subsequent chapters. It also introduces the key ideas about freedom and authority. In the subsequent chapters, the method and questions established with Philemon are carried into the study of 1 Corinthians. The text of 1 Corinthians is examined thematically, opening up questions pertinent to contemporary debates and issues. There are glossary notes on key theological terms, questions for the reader, and suggestions for further reading.

1 Corinthians provides a rich case study in many of the issues that make Paul's letters sites of conflict still today. Free-dom and authority, equality and hierarchy, power and weakness are explicit and endemic issues among the Corinthian Christians and Paul's relationship with them. They impact upon the behaviour of women and men, wives and husbands in the community, on the heads of households and their subordinates, on the congregational worship and common meals, on the relationships of believers with non-believers, and the ideas of leadership and service within the community of Christians. They are also key ideas in the relationship of these believers with Paul. His encouragement to them to 'judge for themselves' is (it is argued in this book) key to the nature of Paul's ministry, and raises questions about the authority he did or did not expect to be granted.

This opens questions too about the authority of Scripture and about the relationship of a Christian today with this letter and with Paul. These ideas form a persistent focus throughout the book and awareness of them is an integral part of the reading strategy being encouraged.

Judge for Yourselves does not offer a detailed commentary on the whole of 1 Corinthians, though parts are studied in some detail, but will be a valuable aid to those seeking an entry into Pauline theology and exegesis. It encourages the reader to grasp the whole letter and to apply similar theological and methodological questions to other Pauline letters.

The New Revised Standard Version is used for quoting the text, except sometimes where different possibilities of translating some words are being discussed.

CHAPTER I

'If you consider me your partner': a case study in Paul's message and method

Philemon

This chapter introduces a strategy for reading a Pauline letter and some of the key theological issues which our study of 1 Corinthians will pursue in subsequent chapters.

Reading letters

If we are reading a letter, and Paul's writings are either real letters or something very like them, we will have expectations about the type of material we are reading and about the style of it. The conventions of the genre of letters in the Roman Empire in the first century will not be entirely those of twenty-first-century Britain but they have a lot in common.

These are communications written by someone at a distance from the individuals or groups who are to receive them. We might have to guess at exactly who these are if the letter just gives us a name or a church community. A letter is written because of factors such as the need to inform or question or warn or encourage or explain. We may know only through the text itself what has occasioned the letter. They are part of the relationship between the writer and recipient(s). We may know only from the writing, the content and the style, whether that relationship is warm or wary, or one of equality or sub-ordination. The correspondence may be part of an exchange of several letters, or after a visit where a number of things were dis-cussed and experienced. We may only have one letter out of such a sequence of letters or events and we will have to make some guesses about what went before.

If, within our own conventions of personal letter-writing, we were to come across a text reading as follows:

Dear Phil,

No, of course you can't. Whatever were you thinking of? As for the other matter, as I said at the time, all's fair in love and war.

Tim says Hello and he'll tell you about what happened at the meeting when he sees you.

Yours, Paul

we might feel fairly limited about what we could construct about the writer, the recipient, their shared understanding, the events and issues referred to. We would not however be wholly bewildered. The content and the style tell us a few things – such as that this is a personal note and not a formal correspondence and is made in response to a previous request from Phil, etc. If for some reason, perhaps from another document, we happened to know something referred to, such as the identity of the 'Tim' mentioned, or details of 'the meeting', we might be able to fit some external facts into the whole picture, to help us 'read the gaps'. If we were literalist, or unaware of the colloquial use of quotations, we might assume, erroneously, that the note was written in time of war. Shared conventions and expectations can be crucial to communication and understanding of speech and text.

📖   Read the letter of Paul to Philemon.

What seems to have been the 'occasion' that caused Paul to write this letter? (Verses 10, 16 & 17 might be key.)

It has not remained a personal letter asking one person for something – now it is in every copy of the New Testament. Why might it have been seen as more than of 'occasional' importance – in what ways might it provide something important to all Christians?

The structure of Paul's letters

Even though most are much longer than letters regularly sent in his day, Paul's letters follow the conventions of the time for formal letters, and have a characteristic pattern. (See, for example, Zeisler 1990, p. 5, drawing on the early work of Deissmann and others; for more detail see, for example, Stowers 1986. Books referred to like this are listed at the end of each chapter.) In Paul's letters, first there is the greeting, then a thanksgiving, then an opening or heading to the body of the letter followed by the body of the letter, and they close with personal greetings and a blessing. The body of the letter is often in two sections: the first can be theoretical teaching and the second practical teaching, often ethical exhortation. For example, Romans 12 opens the 'second part' of that long letter with a 'Therefore . . .' or 'So . . .' which indicates the transition from (in the main) theoretical teaching to (primarily) application and ethics.

A grasp of this pattern can be very helpful in understanding Paul. Philemon is very short so to expect two sections, theoretical and practical, is perhaps unreasonable but try fitting the verses of Philemon into the structure outlined. The paragraphs of the translation you are using may help with some divisions.

Characteristic structure	verses	Outline of Content
Opening: writer, recipient, greeting		
Thanksgiving		
Heading of body of letter		
Body of letter (a) Theoretical part		
Body of letter (b) Practical/ethical part		
Closing: greetings, benediction		

There are particular insights to be gained from an understanding of the structure. We will take a 'section' at a time.

Opening

The way Paul describes himself in the opening greeting of his letters varies from one letter to another and he is often using even this section to make a point which is part of the reason for the letter. For example, in Galatians 1:1 he uses the greeting to describe himself as 'an apostle – sent neither by human commission nor by human authorities' and in that letter he is going to separate himself from the church authorities in Jerusalem and from the views of those like Cephas (Peter) whom he thinks are wrong (Gal. 2:11). The greeting 'sets out his stall'.

📖   Reread Philemon 1–3.

How does Paul describe himself and the people he is writing to? Are they significant terms?

Is he 'setting out his stall' like this in the greeting to Philemon? He calls himself **a prisoner of Christ Jesus** and he will refer to his imprisonment again, in verses 9, 13 and 23. Paul is well able to use double meanings and he may mean both that he is imprisoned *by* Christ and imprisoned *for the sake of* Christ. He is clearly referring physically to his imprisonment (probably in Ephesus) by the civil authorities because of his allegiance to Christ and the preaching of the gospel. He may also be referring metaphorically to being 'captured' by Christ – rather in the way that he also refers to a free believer like himself as **a slave of Christ** (1 Cor. 7:22). The repeated references do seem to be designed to remind the reader that he is in a needy position – he wants something as a result of this letter.

At the same time he reminds his readers that if they value the work of the gospel, they ought to help him because he is suffering on account of it. Right from the start of the letter we might want to start weighing up how far we think Paul is a manipulative writer – the words and phrases he uses influence the way the reader feels. Is this masterly rhetoric or a sort of moral blackmail?

The letter is also said to be from **Timothy our brother**. Paul's letters were probably usually dictated to one of his co-workers who wrote while Paul spoke. It is likely that for this letter Timothy was the 'amanuensis' or secretary, as Sosthenes is for 1 Corinthians (see 1 Cor. 1:1). Would this writer contribute at all to the contents of the letter? It is hard to say. Sometimes Paul apparently took hold of the pen himself in order to make a personal gesture (see Philem. 19). In some portions of letters where Paul is making complex arguments, his sentences do not resolve grammatically, and it may be that dictating, rather than writing, contributes to this style (because when you are writing you can keep what you have written constantly before you). Usually however Paul's prose is very accomplished, and he was clearly used to oral composition. In the same way, most people were used to hearing things read out, rather than reading them for themselves.

The three named people addressed are described as **our beloved co-worker, our sister, our fellow soldier**. Many people guess – but they are guesses – that **Apphia** was **Philemon**'s wife and **Archippus** another member of the household, perhaps their son. Paul regularly addresses believers, as here, as 'brothers and sisters' (as some Christian communities and congregations still do). It indicates intimacy and affection – as the term **beloved** (or **dear friend,** NRSV) does also – but it is also a term that indicates an equality between the members of a community. Households were on the whole very hierarchical, with slaves and masters, and husbands with subordinate wives, and parents who expected obedience from their children. The preference for **sister** and **brother** might indicate an expectation of relationships without that hierarchy. The words **co-worker** and **fellow soldier** (see also **partner** in verse 17) similarly show Paul's understanding that others work alongside him in Christ, rather than merely being under his authority. (More of this in Chapter 5.)

The final greeting does not name an individual but **the church in your house**. The first Christians had no dedicated buildings to meet in (probably not until the third century) but gathered in someone's private house. Archaeology suggests that a villa of a wealthy person, other than the palaces of rulers, would have been unlikely to accommodate more than forty or fifty people (more of this in Chapter 6) so presumably if the church grew larger than this, they would have had to be hosted by more than one household, or meet at different times. The opportunities for factionalism would be present in any such divisions, and we might hold this in mind when we look at some of the issues for the church at Corinth.

Is only the greeting meant to be passed on to the whole congregation or would the whole letter have been read out to them all? In the Greek, the word **you** when it occurs throughout verses 4 to 21 is singular (whereas the **you** and **your** in verse 22 is plural) so on the whole Paul is explicitly addressing Philemon. However, the other letters of Paul that we have were evidently meant for public reading, and this personal letter has ended up in a collection designed for public reading. Also the letter was carried (presumably – see verse 12) by Onesimus himself so the matter would have been known to the whole community. What effect would it have had on Philemon and on the community to hear this letter together? Was it designed to have a message for all of them? Was it a way of putting pressure on Philemon? These are things to bear in mind. Paul's manner (and theology) reflects an expectation of Christians sharing together in many aspects of life. We will see this when we look at the thanksgiving.

Thanksgiving

Paul is following a contemporary style when he tells his readers that he is praying for them, and he almost invariably makes the section after his opening greeting one of thanksgiving. (The exception is the Letter to the Galatians – Paul seems to be so angry that he feels he has no cause to give thanks: see Gal. 1:6–9.) The prayers are not merely general and interchangeable between one letter and another, any more than the greetings are. The thanksgivings are closely targeted to the occasion of the letter and the purpose of his writing. In thanking God for what his readers have done, he is reminding them also of what they will do. The thanksgiving is *the basis for an appeal*. There may be a parallel in the way a sport's coach might encourage a team before a match with praise for how good they are, perhaps more than they truly deserve, in the hope they will then go out and be as good as she says!

📖 Reread Philemon 4–7.

What words does Paul use in this section which he will use again in the rest of the letter?

The echoes of particular words in the rest of the letter are revealing: the words that seem of general application in the thanksgiving are later targeted on the practical effects that Paul is seeking. (It may depend on the translation you are using how many of these you have been able to find: many translations, for good reasons, do not always translate a Greek word with the *same* English word each time it appears.) **Love** in verse 5 will be a key word in the opening of the body of the letter, verse 9. In verse 6, part of the **good** that Paul says he wants Philemon to perceive is made specific in the **good deed** of verse 14. Similarly the **refresh** in verse 7 has a specific application when it is echoed in verse 20.

That there is something emotional and relational is at stake is clear from the **heart(s)** of verse 7, echoed in verses 12 and 20. (The word usually translated **heart** is actually 'bowels'. The idea of the heart as the seat of the emotions, or a metaphor for our emotional centre, is a fairly modern one and the Hebrew view along with much of the ancient world was that we *feel* with our guts. We still talk about a 'visceral' response, and a 'gut reaction'.) **Brother** is also a repeated term – used twice of the relationship between Paul and Philemon (7 and 20) – and these two uses tellingly frame the use of the same word for the relationship that Philemon should now have with Onesimus (16).

One word that is echoed which it is hard for an English translation to demonstrate is the **sharing** (Greek: *koinōnia)* in verse 6 and **partner** (*koinōnon*) in verse 17.

 GLOSSARY : *Koinōnia*

This Greek word is not easy to translate in a single word for every use. It means participation, sharing, a close and mutual relationship. A Christian tradition of translation uses 'fellowship' for *koinōnia*. Paul's great metaphor for this 'common life' in Christ is 'the Body' (see Chapter 8 below on this image used in 1 Cor. 12).

It is a fundamental part of Paul's theology that the believer, while responsible for her or his individual actions, is part of a body of believers. The church is a corporate entity of participation and mutual support, and of shared identity. It has a corporate identity because it identifies with Christ. To be baptised into Christ is to be baptised into his death and resurrection, and be like Christ (Rom. 6:1–11). So, 'we who are many are one body' (1 Cor. 10:17).

This bedrock meaning for Paul of *koinōnia* is a key to other uses of the word. For example, in 2 Cor. 8:4, it refers to a form of almsgiving, a material generosity and sharing. One follows from the other. Christians belong to one another and therefore share goods in common.

Koinōnia is the Greek word behind the phrase 'the fellowship of the Holy Spirit' used in the prayer called 'The Grace' (deriving from 2 Cor. 13:13). It is perhaps an unfortunate ambiguity that 'fellowship' can in English mean something like 'companionableness', so that it seems as if the prayer is for the Holy Spirit to accompany the individual Christian. While this may be a gift of grace to be sought, such a translation can lose the sense that the prayer is for the common life of Christians in the Spirit. The NRSV for 2 Cor. 13:13 translates 'the communion of the Holy Spirit' with a footnote suggesting an alternative, 'the sharing in the Holy Spirit'. These are perhaps better. If 'fellowship' is retained as a translation, the phrase 'the fellowship in the Holy Spirit' might convey a more thoroughly Pauline sense.

The sharing or fellowship that Paul is giving thanks for, and seeking a particular instance of, is the Christian recognition of the common life in Christ. As always with Paul, the fundamental theological principles – like *koinōnia* – are meant to have practical outworking and not remain a mere theory. The reference to Philemon's **sharing** is partly to remind him of the mutual obligations he has in Christ to recognise his kinship with Onesimus, and also with Paul.

This theology of commonality has a bearing on the whole relationship of Paul with his addressees: they are fundamentally his **partners** in Christ, even though they may also be his 'children' (more on this in Chapters 5 and 8 below). He prays for them, and they for him (4 and 22).

Heading

In a letter as short as this, we may not feel a need to isolate one or more verses as distinctively the 'heading' of the body of the letter. It is, however, a thoroughly useful trick to recognise that Paul regularly tells the reader what the whole letter is about at this position in the correspondence. If you get lost in the middle of Romans, for example, it can be useful to keep in mind the verses (Rom. 1:16–17) that follow the thanksgiving as the key or title to the whole. We will later examine if this pattern works well for reading 1 Corinthians.

📖   Reread Philemon 8–10.

Imagine you are reading or hearing this letter for the first time, and this is therefore the first explicit mention you have had of what the letter is about. What strike you as the key words which set out the basis of Paul's appeal? What are the significant 'facts' about the subject of the letter that Paul here first gives the reader?

There is a basic antithesis in verses 8 and 9 between a **command** because of **duty** and an **appeal** because of **love**. Paul refers implicitly later to the idea of a **duty** when he writes (19) that Philemon owes a spiritual debt to Paul, and the idea of a **command** is again implied when he writes of Philemon's **obedience** (21), or even when he mentions the **service** that it is Philemon's place to offer him (12). However, an **appeal on the basis of love** is by far the stronger feature of the language throughout the letter. Paul has already said in the thanksgiving section that he has before this **received much joy and encouragement from** (Philemon's) **love**. We have already noticed the repetition of words like **love** and **heart**.

If verses 8 and 9 might be seen as a summary of what Paul says is his *method* – **appeal** not **command** – verse 10 might be seen as an encapsulation of the *message*. The subject of the appeal is Onesimus, and the first thing we hear about him – the thing Paul wants to highlight about him – is the child-father relationship that he now has with Paul. This is a metaphor Paul uses elsewhere (e.g. 1 Cor. 4:15) about his relationship with the people he has brought to belief in Christ. Interestingly this does not diminish the fundamental brother/sister relationship that Paul has with the same people (Philem. 16). Onesimus' conversion, and Paul's valuing of Onesimus, are going to be key to what the letter is about.

That Paul is **bold enough in Christ to command** is part of an important discussion in Pauline theology. There is a persistent theme – sometimes an undercurrent and sometimes explicit – in Paul's letters of the question of his authority, and of all Christian authority. One thing at stake is the independence of his authority from the leaders of the Jerusalem churches. There were clearly those who denied his apostleship (1 Cor. 9:2). These issues will be pursued in Chapter 5 below, and throughout.

Body of the letter (a)

Most scholars reconstruct the events behind the letter, as you too
have probably done, on the assumption that Onesimus was a slave in
Philemon's household who had escaped, possibly with some stolen
goods (18), had somehow come in touch with Paul, and become a
Christian. However, this is not a wholly unproblematic reading.

First, was it merely a (huge) coincidence that Onesimus found
Paul in Ephesus (or Rome – scholars are divided on the location)? He
could hardly have bumped into another person with a closer, more
significant relationship with his owner. Second, Roman laws were
severe both for runaway slaves and for the people who assisted them,
whereas Paul seems able to treat this as a matter of *personal* reconciliation. This illustrates that we may not be able to be certain about
some factual details.

You may even have noticed that Paul does not say anywhere in the
letter that Onesimus has run away. It is a perfectly reasonable construction, perhaps the best construction, of what is implied, but it is
actually just one 'reading of the gaps'. More than one scholar has
suggested that Onesimus had undertaken a legitimate journey to Paul
and that Paul, having led him into faith, wanted him to stay on to
assist him: the letter asks for Onesimus to be welcomed as a
Christian brother and sent back to assist Paul further.

It is important to recognise that we cannot always be sure about
some things in our texts: we look to make sense of them, but then we
need to check the sense that we have made against the details of the
text and against background information, such as the nature of
slavery in the Roman Empire. It is often useful to consider more than
one possibility.

Reread Philemon 11–16.

Let us assume that the usual structure of some of Paul's longer
letters is also reflected here, and that there is a theoretical base
before the practical application. If we regard these verses as
articulating the theoretical or theological basis of what Paul wants
Philemon to do, what phrases in them express a principle?

Whatever the circumstances, the appeal seems to be driven by two things which give a theoretical, theological base to the letter. One is the worth of Onesimus. He was useful to Paul. There is a pun in verse 11 and possibly in 20: the name Onesimus was often given to a slave because it means 'useful'. Moreover, as a believer he should now be received as a beloved brother by his owner. Secondly, there is the importance given to the voluntary, consenting response of Philemon. Both of these refer back to the 'heading': **I would rather appeal on the basis of love**.

We noted that Paul can exhibit concern about his own authority. At the same time, his theology is fundamentally based not on command, rights and status, but on grace, freedom and love. It matters to him that Philemon should respond to his request freely out of love because that is how, for him, the gospel works. The evangelist John has been called 'the Apostle of Love' but, arguably, Paul has as much claim to the title.

Body of the letter (b)

We may or may not decide that the main body of this letter divides into theoretical and practical halves, but we can still see how Paul articulates both the principle(s) behind what he exhorts and how he is explicit about the outworking and application of the principles. He is a thoroughly 'applied' or 'practical' theologian. He has overarching theological principles which he can relate to the most mundane things – and relate mundane things to those principles. (We will see examples of this in 1 Corinthians.)

📖   Reread Philemon 17–21.

Notice the number of exhortations in this section – list the things Paul wants Philemon to do. What is implied in verse 21?

Paul's style in this section makes him vulnerable to the charge of those readers who find him manipulative. When (19) he writes **I say nothing about your owing me even your own self**, he is employing a common rhetorical device where a writer or speaker protests that s/he will *not* say something, and in doing so, says it! It is probably important to recognise that Paul does indeed believe that the gift of grace that Philemon has received is immeasurable, and that he knows Philemon believes this too. It is worth his mentioning it, because it is just this gift of grace which has now come to Onesimus too, and any debt between slave and master is now of infinitesimal significance measured against the free gift of grace. (The theology is like that in Jesus' parable of the ungrateful slave in Matthew 18:21–35.)

The tension of freedom and obedience, introduced in the heading to the body of the letter, returns in the final verse, 21, of the body of the letter. Here again free gift and consent are seen as something more than obedience. When Paul says that Philemon will do **more** than he asks for, does he have something specific in mind? Does he expect Philemon to give Onesimus his freedom? The silence of Paul (and the whole of the New Testament) on the evils of institutional slavery is problematic – we will look at this again in Chapter 10. Another guess is that Paul wants Philemon not only to welcome Onesimus but to send him back again to be **useful** to Paul.

Though there was no public mail service in the Empire, communication routes were good and many people travelled. The grain ships could be used for journeys by sea, and the Egnatian Way linked major cities in Asia Minor by land. Letters, however, had to be carried by hand and someone had to make an expensive, and sometimes dangerous, journey to take a letter. Therefore we do not have in the written letter the whole of the messages that passed on these occasions between Paul and his churches: someone brought the letter and could speak about Paul's views and give other information. On this occasion it is evidently Onesimus himself who brings the letter and – surely – had views himself on what he wanted to happen!

Incidentally, matters like these have a bearing on things like the dating and location of the letters. If Paul wants Onesimus to return from Colossae after delivering this letter, it might seem more likely that the letter is written from Ephesus than from Rome. The journey from Rome to Colossae and back would involve expense and danger, and one might expect Paul to have sent someone else with the message, who would not, as he seems to hope Onesimus would, be coming directly back. Ephesus and Colossae are comparatively close. Different scholars take different views on this sort of matter of the dating and location of Paul's letters, based partly on speculative arguments like this.

Closing

📖 Reread Philemon 22–25.

What echoes are here of words (or ideas) from the rest of the letter?

Reflecting on the message and the method

There is no doubt that Paul writes in order to persuade. His rhetorical devices often call for a response from the reader – he hopes to bring his readers to share his opinion. Paul writes that he will not **command** Philemon to do as he asks because he wants Philemon to act freely and not in response to his authority. This appears to leave Philemon free to choose, but does it? Also, the letter greets the whole church so would have been read out publicly: under what pressure would that put Philemon? As readers of any text, we can ask not only 'What is the writer saying?' but 'What is the writer doing?' (an approach sometimes called 'a hermeneutics of suspicion'). We should include in our reflections the realisation that the sending of the letter is itself an act of authority. Is Paul manipulative? His personality comes across (to me) as passionate rather than calculating. He certainly was, and is, very persuasive.

Paul is passionately committed to the people to whom he writes – these are, in a sense, love letters. Apart from the letter to the Romans, all the surviving letters are written to churches Paul has visited and probably founded. He knows these people; he has brought them to faith in Christ and thinks of himself, sometimes, as their father. They are the letters of a pastor, trying to maintain a pastoral role at a distance.

I headed this chapter with the quotation (Philem. 17) **'If you consider me your partner'**. This is in part because I see the theology of *koinōnia*, Christian participation, as central to the message and method of the letter. It is also because I would like to maintain a focus in this book on Paul's sharing and expectation of *participation with his readers*. That applies first and foremost to his intended readers, Philemon, the congregations of Corinth, etc. It might also be an interesting reading strategy for us.

Paul's letters are open to the operation of the reader as a partner in exploring and applying theology. Paul rarely gives instructions as unassailable and unexplained edicts. He argues from theological principles in an attempt to persuade. **Judge for yourselves**, he says twice in 1 Corinthians (10:15; 11:13).

Persuasion is only ever necessary when more than one view is possible on a subject – Paul is very aware that his correspondents may sometimes disagree. We will see that his correspondents in Corinth, for a time, do indeed seem to have been unconvinced by his arguments (Chapter 2 below).

Because his theology is engaged with real Christian communities, applied to situations, part of the role of the reader as partner with Paul can be to consider what it means to do the same. I am thinking here of Christian readers today of the letters. By 'consider what it means to do the same', I do not mean that the reader is to read what Paul says, and carry out an instruction in Christian living without regard to the real community, the actual situation in which it is to be applied. Rather, the reader as partner might apply the principles to different situations, and in so doing will make different decisions about *what is the action that fulfils the theological principle at stake.*

In this strategy of reading, Paul says to the reader, 'Consider me your partner', and the reader can engage with the letter not so much to do what Paul *says,* but to do what he *does.* This idea will be revisited in the final chapter.

Suggestions for further reading

Donfried, Karl P. and Marshall, I.H., 1993. *The Theology of the Shorter Pauline Letters*, Cambridge, CUP

Fitzmyer, Joseph A., 1993. 'Introduction to the New Testament Epistles' in R.E. Brown *et al.* (eds.), *The New Jerome Biblical Commentary* (Study Ed.), London, Geoffrey Chapman

Minear, Paul S., 1993. 'Philemon, The Letter of Paul to', in B.M. Metzger *et al.* (eds.), *The Oxford Companion to the Bible*, Oxford, OUP, pp. 589–90.

O'Brien, Peter T., 1982. *Word Biblical Commentary: Colossians and Philemon*, Waco, Texas, Word Books

Wright, N.T., 1986. *Tyndale New Testament Commentaries: Colossians and Philemon*, Leicester, IVP

Zeisler, John, 1990 (revised). *Pauline Christianity*, Oxford, OUP

In this chapter, reference was also made to the following works

Stowers, Stanley K., 1986. *Letter-Writing in Greco-Roman Antiquity*, Philadelphia, Westminster

CHAPTER 2

'I appeal to you': applying the questions to 1 Corinthians

1 Corinthians 1

This chapter will look at the structure of the whole of 1 Corinthians, as demonstrated in Chapter 1 using Philemon. It will also look ahead to what happened after the letter was sent, by examining parts of 2 Corinthians. The first chapter of 1 Corinthians will be studied in more detail in order to open up the particularities of the letter, the church, the issues, but we will read the whole letter and attempt to get a holistic sense of Paul's message. This will give us a 'first impression' to test against the different parts of the letter in later chapters below.

Distance learning

1 Corinthians is among other things a testimony to Paul the pastor, seeking to guide and nurture one of his communities of believers while apart from them. The Christian Church has had many models of ministry since then, some itinerant (like some missionaries), some regional (like diocesan bishops), some local (like parish priests). Today, some denominations in Britain have experience of 'church-planting' – establishing communities of Christians in areas such as new housing estates. The relationship of these new churches to the 'mother church', or to a key evangelist from that church, may go through a number of stages. There is likely to be some sense of the church's growing – in numbers or in institutional maturity or in local leadership – and needing to be sponsored, assisted, taught by those who founded and who foster the new church.

This developing relationship must have been even more crucial in a religious movement as new as Christianity was in its first twenty years. At this stage in his relationship with the community in Corinth, Paul is responding to questions they have addressed to him since his visit, and to other things he has heard about their faith and actions. As we try to trace the questions or statements and responses between writer and first readers, we need to keep the recent founding of the church in mind. The Corinthians have questions about their new faith and new way of life that arise in part from Paul's own original procla-mation to them. Some of their concerns may arise from the teaching of other missionaries and pastors, but the bulk of the correspon-dence, an ongoing dialogue between the church and its founding pastor, may reflect in large measure the substance of Paul's own first teaching to them.

The Corinthian correspondence – first stage

Paul refers in passing (1 Cor. 1:14–16; 2:1–5) to his time in Corinth when he made converts of those to whom he now writes. Other teachers, Apollos and perhaps Cephas (Peter), have visited them since. The narrative in the Acts of the Apostles provides confirmation of some details of the founding of this church (Acts 18:1–7). It also helps us to date the visit to about 50–51 CE, because the Gallio who is mentioned in Acts 18:12 was proconsul during those years. (We know this because of an inscription discovered in Delphi; see, e.g., Holladay 1993, p. 135.) Paul now writes from Ephesus (1 Cor. 16:8), perhaps in 53 or 54 CE.

📖 Read I Corinthians 2:1; 5:9; 7:1; 16:5–7, 8, 10, 12, 17 and also 1:11.

What can you trace in these verses of the interaction, past, present and projected, between Paul and the believers in Corinth?

We learn from 1 Corinthians 5:9 that what we are reading is not really 'the *First* Letter of Paul to the Corinthians' at all. Paul has written before, and one of the things this earlier letter said was that the believers should not associate with sexually immoral persons. Commentators sometimes refer to this as the 'puritanical' letter (e.g. in Barrett 1971) though sexual morality continues as one issue between Paul and his converts in later letters also (1 Cor. 5:1–13; 6:9–20). It is just possible that we actually have a fragment of this letter, hidden away in 2 Corinthians. Misplaced manuscript fragments have sometimes been interpolated into another document and then copied in subsequent versions as if they were part of that work.

📖   Read 2 Corinthians 6:11–13 and then jump straight to 7:2–4.

Would you have noticed, in terms of sense, that 6:14–7:1 was missed out?

📖   Read 2 Corinthians 6:14–7:1.

Is there anything here that might suggest this could be a small part of the same letter Paul refers to in 1 Corinthians 5:9?

We then learn (1 Cor. 7:1) that there has also been a letter from the Corinthian believers to Paul. This we certainly do not have, alas, but the repetition of **Now concerning** . . . (7:1, 25; 8:1; 12:1; 16:1, 12) may indicate that Paul is answering the previous letter point by point, so we might be able to reconstruct its questions.

A letter must have been carried by someone, and in 16:17 Paul rejoices at the arrival of Stephanas, Fortunatus and Achaicus: did these men bring the letter? Did they add to it any commentary of their own which informs or influences Paul's response? When Paul asks, **[H]ow can some of you say that there is no resurrection** . . . (15:12), how does he know this? Was it in a letter? Did one of the travellers bring this report? Other people have been messengers too. **Chloe's people** have reported to Paul that there are quarrels among the Christians at Corinth (1:11). What else did they say? Chloe is presumably a believer wealthy enough to have household servants or slaves, and to send them on journeys. Did they travel with Stephanas and the others? Stephanas and the others are presumably not **Chloe's people** because Stephanas has a household of his own (1:16).

The letter is by no means intended as a conclusion of Paul's mentoring of this congregation. He plans to use colleagues to maintain his relationship with them and to provide for their further guidance. Timothy may visit them on his way to Paul (16:10) and Paul also wants Apollos to do so (16:12). Paul himself plans to visit as part of a trip that will take in other congregations too (16:5).

The Corinthian correspondence – second stage

Though Paul does make such a visit, apparently all does not go well between him and his correspondents.

📖   Read 2 Corinthians 1:15–16, 23–2:1, 3–4; 7:8, 5, 15, 6–7 (in this order).

These verses may help us construct a chronological sequence of events after the Corinthian believers had received the letter that we call 1 Corinthians. Try to trace what has happened in the relationship between Paul and the Corinthians. Who visited whom, who wrote to whom, and what was the result at each stage?

Paul does indeed make a visit, and not, as he first planned according to 1 Corinthians 16, *after* he has travelled through Macedonia but *before* this, so that he can visit them a further time on his way back to Ephesus again. This **painful visit** (2 Cor. 2:1) makes him decide not to go through Corinth on the return trip. Something happens that creates a serious rift between them. Was it in part that they did not respond positively to something in the letter we call 1 Corinthians? Paul writes again in a distressed frame of mind (2 Cor. 2:3–4 and 7:8) in such a way as to cause pain to his correspondents. (Some commentators think we have part of this severe letter misplaced or collated into 2 Corinthians as chapters 10–13.)

It is not clear how the great affliction Paul writes of in 2 Corinthians 1:8–9 is related to this rift – it takes place in Asia (where Ephesus is located) and not in Macedonia where the next phase in the relationship takes place. Paul describes his situation as **disputes without and fears within** (7:5) as he travels into Macedonia, but it seems that Titus had been received by the Corinthians as Paul's emissary, and that he returned to Paul with news of their desire for reconciliation. Paul's letter had given them pain, but had some effect in bringing about repentance and reconciliation. And so Paul writes the letter we call 2 Corinthians – or at least what is now the bulk of 2 Corinthians 1–9.

Although 2 Corinthians is not to be the major focus of our study in this book, the later stage of the correspondence is illuminating in a number of ways. It suggests that 1 Corinthians did not achieve Paul's desired ends – we might need to think of the first readers as not agreeing with all that Paul writes in this letter. The later story also illustrates further the passion in the relationship between this pastor and his flock.

The structure of Paul's letters

📖 Read I Corinthians at one sitting.

Now identify the sections with which Paul usually structures his letters: Opening, Thanksgiving, Heading, Body of the letter, Closing – following the grid in Chapter I above. Don't worry at this stage about dividing the body of the letter into (a) theoretical and (b) practical, unless such a pattern is clear to you.

Opening

📖 Reread I Corinthians 1:1–3.

If Paul consciously uses even the greeting to begin to make his points, what do these verses tell us about what he wants the Corinthians to reflect on about himself, and about their own condition?

There is a word used twice in this greeting: Paul says he is **called** to be an apostle (more of this in Chapter 5) and that the believers are **called** to be **saints**. Followers of Christ were not at first known as 'Christians', and **saints** is one of Paul's common collective terms for them. (It is always used in the plural in the New Testament – that is, no individual is known by the word as a title, like 'Saint Peter' or 'Saint Paul', until later in the Church's history.) However, Paul emphasises the term here with another descriptive phrase, using the related word **sanctified**. He does seem to be reminding them of a common call to holiness. Is this going to be part of the substance of the letter?

The second half of his description of them seems to hint at something significant also. Why does he remind them that they are not the only followers of Christ? Is the church here believing or practising something that makes them different from other churches? In later sections, look out for places where Paul refers them to what other churches do (e.g. 11:16; 14:36).

Thanksgiving

📖   Reread I Corinthians 1:4–9.

Remember that the ideas in the Thanksgiving often reflect the basis of Paul's appeal. What characteristics of the believers in Corinth does Paul make the most of here? Is there a hidden warning in his praise? Are there any words in the Thanksgiving that Paul also used in the Greeting?

The thankfulness that Paul says he has for the believers in Corinth is about the **spiritual gifts** they have been given, gifts of **speech** and **knowledge**. It seems likely (e.g. from 1 Cor. 8, and 11–14) that this is a community that enjoys and prizes some particular charismatic gifts (more about these in Chapter 8). Paul by no means discourages these – he is giving thanks – but he seems to want to introduce the idea of **the end**. (We will look at Paul's ideas about the end of the world in Chapter 4.) He hints that it is not enough for them to have these gifts but that there needs to be some perseverance and some strengthening, and dependence on the faithfulness of God. Remember that in the Greeting they were **sanctified** and **called to be saints**. Here they are again reminded of God's call to them and the requirement to be **blameless**. Together, these hints amount to quite a strong warning that Paul does not think that all there is to do is give thanks for the giftedness of this congregation. And of course, if that were so, there would have been little need for him to send a letter at all.

The very end of the Thanksgiving leads Paul into his opening. Paul writes (1:9) that the believers are called into **the fellowship** of Christ. This is *koinōnia* again. By this, he may be hinting at the requirement for sharing and common life among the believers in Corinth, for we quickly learn that there are divisions among them.

Heading

📖   Reread I Corinthians 1:10.

From your reading of the whole letter, how well does this verse function as a heading, a summary, of the whole contents? Is this what all the parts of the letter are about?

Body of the letter (a)

📖   Reread I Corinthians I:11–31.

If what Paul begins to write about here is a direct response to what members of Chloe's household reported to him, can you reconstruct any of the particulars about which Chloe's people told him?

What is Paul's key theological teaching in responding to the situation?

Exactly what the Corinthians thought they meant if they said, **I belong to** one of the Church's missionaries or teachers is not known to us. What is clear is that Paul is appalled by it. His question, **Has Christ been divided?** (1:13), is a shocking way of putting it. He uses the metaphor of the Body of Christ to speak of believers collectively and that idea must lie behind the question, but on the face of it the question asks if Christ himself has been dismembered, cut up.

His theology is not just about the believers' unity in Christ but their salvation through the cross of Christ. For Paul a person's baptism into Christ is a baptism, mystically, in the *death* of Christ – a sharing in that death in order to share also the new life of the resurrection. (He doesn't spell this out here in these terms, but other passages such as Romans 6:3–11 can help us to grasp his theology.)

🗁   GLOSSARY : *Christ crucified*

When Paul writes, 'We proclaim Christ crucified' (I Cor. 1:23), or about the 'power' of 'the cross of Christ' (1:17), what does he mean?

Christos is a Greek word which is a translation of the Hebrew word *Messiah*, and they mean 'anointed'. This is a metaphor deriving from the ritual practice of anointing certain individuals with oil to designate them as people with a special function to perform, and in Jewish tradition it denotes their appointment for this function by God.

In the Old Testament priests, patriarchs and kings are anointed or referred to as 'anointed' (Lev. 4:3; I Sam. 10:1; I Chron. 16:22). With the promise made to David that the rule of his descendants would be established 'for ever' (2 Sam. 7:12f.), the Davidic dynasty came to be regarded as especially chosen by God. After the return from exile in Babylon, the descendants of the house of David did not rule the nation: the later rulers, the Hasmonaeans, were descended from the High Priests rather than from David's line. Nevertheless one of the strands of Jewish expectation of salvation from God still centred on the hope of a king who would be both 'a son of David' and 'the Lord's anointed'.

The New Testament identifies the fulfilment of this expectation in Jesus of Nazareth (see e.g. Matt. 2:4–6; Mark 10:47; Luke 2:11). Jesus himself is recorded as accepting, or at least not rejecting, the title of 'Christ' (e.g. Mark 8:29; 14:61f.) though it appears not to have been his preferred self-description.

His use of the ambiguous phrase 'the son of man' for himself is much more characteristic, and this might be in keeping with a reluctance to see his mission as fulfilling all the expectations that some of his contemporaries may have had about 'the Messiah'. For example, there was sometimes, in occupied Palestine, a heightened expectation at Passover time of the Messiah's acting to liberate God's people. This reflected the role of Moses as God's appointed leader of the Israelites in liberating them from Egypt. John's Gospel records Jesus withdrawing from the crowds, near the time of Passover, because 'Jesus realised that they were about to come and take him by force to make him king' (John 6:15). There was something in some messianic expectation that Jesus avoided or sought to reinterpret.

The messianic claim was clearly key in the charges that brought Jesus to his death: 'the inscription of the charge against him read, "The King of the Jews" ' (Mark 15:26). The writers of the texts which have become the New Testament very quickly seem to use the title 'Christ' as if it is part of Jesus' name – it is an inseparable part of the belief about Jesus.

However, there was nothing like a developed expectation that God's Messiah would arrive only to be put to a criminal's death. After the crucifixion, when two disciples are met by the risen Christ (Luke 24:13–27), they speak about the *defeat* of their expectation: 'We had hoped that he was the one to redeem Israel' (Luke 24:21). They need further insight and explanation before they can begin to apprehend the idea of a 'suffering' Messiah.

The circumstances of Jesus' death compounded the apparently unmessianic nature of his mission. Death by crucifixion, under Roman Law, was the punishment thought fit for, as it was perceived, the low-life of criminality: robbers, traitors, deserters and rebels. Jesus was deemed guilty by the trial before

Pilate, effectively, of being a rebel against the state. One of the purposes of this form of execution was the public humiliation of those condemned; the intention was to degrade as well as to torture and kill.

Small wonder then that Paul writes (1 Cor. 1:23) that the proclamation of a crucified Messiah is 'a stumbling block to Jews and foolishness to Gentiles.' Paul's own first opposition (see, e.g. Gal. 1:13) to the Church which proclaimed Jesus as Messiah, was surely closely tied to his finding the crucifixion of Jesus a huge stumbling block to any possibility of believing him to be God's anointed. It was even written in the Torah, 'anyone hung on a tree is under God's curse' (Deut. 21:22).

The revelation Paul had of the risen Jesus (see e.g. Gal. 1:15f.) changed his mind so completely that it is precisely 'Christ crucified' that becomes the centre of his message of salvation. In Galatians he refers to the curse on those hanged in Deuteronomy and says that redemption is in this, that 'Christ ... [became] a curse for us' (Gal. 3:13).

Exactly *how* the cross of Christ achieves salvation for others is never really spelled out by Paul or any other New Testament writer. Theologians in the later Church worked out this 'doctrine of the atonement' more systematically, using the insights from New Testament authors including Paul. Paul has a number of ways of speaking of the atonement, using various metaphors: the language of the Temple sacrifices (Rom. 3:25), legal language of acquittal in a court of law (Rom. 4:6ff.), legal language of the manumission (redemption) of slaves (1 Cor. 7:22f.), battle language (1 Cor. 15:24ff.), language of birth and adoption (Gal. 4:4ff.; Rom. 8:22f.), and ambassadorial language of the reconciliation of nations (2 Cor. 5:18–20). The fixed points are that the atonement is an act of God's grace received through faith, and that it is the cross of Christ that reveals or effects it.

The proclamation of the crucifixion of Jesus as Messiah is clearly the most important thing that Paul has to preach. He very rarely refers to any teaching of Jesus (only three times explicitly – discussed in Chapter 3) and never to Gospel narratives of the miracles or parables, the things that the Gospels (written later than Paul's letters) now tell us about. He refers often to Jesus' death.

There is something in this utter reversal of expectation, and the revelation of God's power and wisdom in a moment of degradation and defeat, that motivates the whole Pauline mission and is the mainspring of his theology. For the importance in Paul's theology of the resurrection as well as the crucifixion, see Chapter 4 below.

In 1 Corinthians 1:26–31, Paul applies the reversal of power and weakness, wisdom and foolishness, which he sees in the crucified Messiah, to the believers at Corinth. Paul, even in the height or depth of his theological teaching, rarely or never loses sight of the *situation* that calls forth this expression of his theology. Once again he refers to a **call**, just as he does twice in the opening greeting. This repeated reflection on their first reception of faith reinforces the idea that Paul wants to *recall* them from some divergence from belief or practice. The exaltation here of foolishness and weakness (after the pattern of the cross) suggests that there is in the congregation some sort of claim to wisdom or power or nobility. It seems to be some sort of **boasting** (1 Cor. 3:21) which centres on allegiance to Paul or Apollos or Cephas.

📖   Read I Corinthians 2–4.

Make a note of all the expressions in these chapters which reinforce the reversals of weakness and strength, value and worthlessness.

Note also the various references to Christ. Paul writes (2:2), **I decided to know nothing among you except Christ, and him crucified**. Can you find evidence in these chapters that **Christ crucified** is the key idea in Paul's teaching about how he and the Corinthian believers should behave?

Body of the letter (b)

📖   Reread the first few verses of each chapter from I Corinthians 5–16.

Can you infer from these verses the various issues, questions and situations that Paul addresses in turn?

We only have Paul's writing style to tell us when he had finished with one topic and started on another. The chapter and verse divisions are not original: the Bible wasn't divided into the chapters we have in ours until the thirteenth century. The same is true of paragraphs, which are the later editors' and translators' ideas of divisions of sense in the text.

Your list of the topics will probably include a specific instance of sexual immorality (1 Cor. 5), a believer having a lawsuit against a fellow believer (6), the relationships of married people (7), the eating of food that has been offered to idols (8 and 10), the behaviour of women and men in worship (11), behaviour at the Lord's Supper (11), spiritual gifts in congregational worship (12 and 14), the doctrine of the resurrection of the dead (15), and a collection of money for the believers in Jerusalem (16).

This seems a wide-ranging list of topics. Some readers of this letter think that the usual structure of Paul's letters, where the body of the letter is often in two sections (theoretical teaching followed by practical teaching with ethical exhortation), is not used here. They find that the letter instead addresses a series of issues in turn with a fusion of theoretical and practical teaching.

While there probably is something of this character to the letter, Paul's usual way of writing may still be informing the compositional structure. If the first issue (1 Cor. 1:10–4:21) was about divisions among the believers, and a boasting about human leaders (3:21), is the theological teaching in this section relevant to the issues that follow? I suggested that we could take seriously Paul's claim here that his teaching centred on (and only on) **Christ crucified**, and the theology that God's **power** and **wisdom** is effective in **weakness** and **foolishness**. Is this theology one which is applied to the various topics he addresses later on?

As you read different chapters or sections of the letter in more detail, keep a lookout for words and phrases that echo or apply those teachings of Paul about **Christ crucified** in 1 Corinthians 1. There are two themes to research. One is the exhortation to unity and agreement: **Has Christ been divided?** (1 Cor. 1:13). The other is the great mystery of the reversal: **God's foolishness is wiser than human wisdom, and God's weakness is stronger than human strength**. Paul sees the theology of the cross as one which has direct and practical application in the attitude and behaviour of believers. He will exhort the Corinthians to give way to one another and to seek the advantage not of themselves but of others, because this is the pattern of their salvation, the imitation of Christ. Paul's theology of the cross leads to a voluntary submission of believers for the sake of others. We will investigate this theology further in Chapter 3 below, and look at examples of it in each of the chapters that follow.

Closing

Reread I Corinthians 16:5–24.

What impression do you get from these verses about Paul's relationship with his correspondents?

Can you identify in these final messages and greetings any of the themes and issues which we found in the Opening, Thanksgiving, Heading or Body of the letter? Especially, are there exhortations for them to submit to one another, or references to doing things for the sake of others?

Reflecting on the message and the method

It may seem illogical to have started to look at this letter, not just with a focused study of its first chapter, but with a method that has ranged over the whole of the letter and even parts of 2 Corinthians as well. What we are engaged in is sometimes called the 'hermeneutical circle' (hermeneutics means 'interpretation'). The circle is between the whole and the parts: we cannot understand the whole of a text until we have understood its various parts; yet we cannot understand those parts until we have an understanding of the whole text, and therefore the role the parts play within the whole. The hermeneutical circle or cycle of interpretation is one where we try to get an impression of the whole text. We then test that impression out by examining a part or parts of the text. This might modify, or reinforce, our ideas of what the whole text means so we return to the whole and test out our revised impression.

This sounds impossibly laborious but it is what any reader is consciously or sub-consciously doing all the time. If you read a detective novel, a particular episode may strike you as the key to solving the whole thing. When you reach the end and the detective reveals the final solution, you may have to revise your reading of that episode because the whole plot was not what you expected. We understand the parts by the whole and the whole by the parts.

This is what we shall be doing with 1 Corinthians. It was easier with Philemon because it is so short that we can fairly easily hold the parts and the whole together. 1 Corinthians is longer and ranges over a range of theological and social issues.

I may be wrong that Paul's theology of the cross, with its exhortation to submit to other people's needs in the pattern of Christ crucified, is the interpretative key to the whole letter and its various parts. That is what you can test in the chapters that follow. The idea may need revising, or rejecting, or it may be confirmed.

✎   When you read a biblical text, how far are you prepared to change your mind about what you think particular verses mean when you put it in the context of the whole book or letter? Have your first impressions ever proved mistaken?

✎   You have now read the whole letter, and some parts of it in more detail. Record a summary of what you think the letter is about, what Paul's relationship is like with his correspondents, and what you think are key ideas in Paul's theology. You will then have a record to return to at the end of this study and will be able to see how far you have revised or confirmed your initial opinion.

Suggestions for further reading

Banks, Robert, 1980. *Paul's Idea of Community: the early house churches in their historical setting*, Exeter, Paternoster Press

Barrett, C.K., 1973. *The Second Epistle to the Corinthians*, London, A. and C. Black, pp. 1–20

Dunn, James D.G., 1995. *1 Corinthians: New Testament Guides*, Sheffield, Sheffield Academic Press

Frör, Hans, 1995. *YouWretched Corinthians!: the correspondence between the Church in Corinth and Paul*, trans. J. Bowden, London, SCM

Holladay, Carl R., 1993. 'Corinthians, The Letters of Paul to the', in B.M. Metzger *et al.* (eds.), *The Oxford Companion to the Bible*, Oxford, OUP, pp. 135–8

CHAPTER 3

'The Son himself will be subjected': the servant-sovereignty of Christ

1 Corinthians 15:1–11 and 8:4–6

Paul's letters are fundamentally about the new life in Christ. He uses the word **Christ** no less than ten times in the first ten verses of 1 Corinthians. In this chapter, we will explore Paul's Christology, the bedrock of his language about freedom and authority and subordination. Paul is supremely conscious of the paradox of the **weakness** and **foolishness** of the cross of Christ revealing the **power** and **wisdom** of God. Paul says he proclaims **Christ crucified** but he also proclaims, **Jesus is Lord**.

Lord or servant

What do we mean when we say 'Christianity'? Here is one image that might come into some minds: robed bishops stand in the ancient architectural splendours of Westminster Abbey in the presence of members of the Government and sundry titled persons, while an archbishop places a priceless crown on the head of a new queen or king. Since the conversion of the Emperor Constantine in the fourth century, triumphalist occasions like this have been part of Christianity, in some countries, and the Church has been allied, variously, with the power of secular governments, their laws and their armies.

Here's another image. A member of the congregation of St Andrew's, a suburban parish church, is sorting clothes and bed linen in the laundry of the local hospice as one of their weekend volunteers. There are probably local humanists and Buddhists and others on that volunteer-rota too, but this particular person has chosen to undertake this unobtrusive, not especially sacrificial, task once a month as part of what for her or him is a Christian life.

Is one of these images more representative of Christianity than the other? In the Book of Revelation, there is a vision of Christ receiving the homage of all beings in creation ('every creature in heaven and on earth and under the earth and in the sea') and some of them sing: 'Worthy is the Lamb that was slaughtered to receive power and wealth and wisdom and might and honour and glory and blessing!' (Rev. 5:12). On the other hand, there is a passage in Mark's Gospel where Jesus tells his followers:

> 'You know that among the Gentiles those whom they recognize as their rulers lord it over them, and their great ones are tyrants over them. But it is not so among you; but whoever wishes to become great among you must be your servant, and whoever wishes to be first among you must be slave of all. For the Son of Man came not to be served but to serve . . .' (Mark 10:42–5)

Christianity has a Christ who is enthroned in glory and a Jesus who washes his friends' feet (John 13). If these passages, and the images of Christianity today sketched above, are true reflections of *something* about Christianity, what have they got in common? What can possibly hold them together? The Lordship of the exalted Christ leads to one set of ideas, and the teaching and example of servanthood of Jesus of Nazareth seems to lead to another. How does Paul hold together **Jesus is Lord** with Christ **crucified for you**?

A number of commentators (e.g. Bultmann 1976, pp. 331, 351; Martin 1990, pp. 56f) have pointed out that the term 'Lord' is understandable only in terms of what someone is 'lord' of – that is, a slave or a servant. They are correlative terms and their meaning is mutually interdependent. The understanding of exactly what it meant to be a servant or a slave in the society of the day informs the understanding of what it means to be 'lord'. We will look at Paul's use of the word 'slave' and some of what it meant for him in Chapter 10.

In this chapter we need to put together some of the things that Paul writes about Christ to see if it is a coherent Christology and to see how it relates to the rest of his teaching.

 GLOSSARY : *Christology*

Christology is the study of the person and role of Christ. In Christian doctrine the weight of christologi- cal discussion tends to be on the union of divine and human natures in Christ, with the use of phrases such as 'fully human and fully divine'.

Such language reflects philosophical categories of thought and arguments about the nature of Christ in the second century, rather than the language of the New Testament. One of the most fruitful texts for the doctrinal developments was John 1:1–14, speaking of the incarnation of 'the Word of God'.

We need to be careful of anachronism in reading back later credal statements of the Church into New Testament texts; and of reading the expressions and understanding of one later New Testament text (e.g. Gospel of John) into another New Testament text (e.g. a letter of Paul). All these expressions and understandings may be coherent but they are not identical.

The New Testament texts are thoroughly christological but not *systematically* so. We might characterise the Gospels as 'narrative Christology' or Paul's letters as 'pastoral Christology'. Paul's primary purpose is not to make credal or defensive statements about the person of Christ, though the needs of his congregations may call for teaching about Christ that is relevant to their situation.

A key christological feature of the New Testament texts is the titles given to Jesus – 'Christ', 'Lord', 'Son of God', 'the son of man'. There is a conceptual background to these terms in Jewish and primitive Christian traditions; and there is a cultural context for some of them in Hellenistic society too. When a New Testament author uses one of these, he *may* mean what the later church creeds mean by them, but they may have a different range of meaning.

For example, it is sometimes argued that the 'divine and human natures' of Christ are described respectively by the two New Testament phrases, 'Son of God' (divine nature) and 'the son of man' (human nature). A New Testament author *might* use them in this way but the titles are open to quite different meanings and are actually as likely to function the opposite way around: 'the son of man' seems to refer to a figure who comes from heaven with divine authority in Daniel 7:13, while 'son of God' could mean a human agent of God like King David (2 Sam. 7:14).

The Church's Christology eventually defined the person of Christ in terms of Trinitarian theology and refers to Jesus as 'God the Son'. One insight may lead to the other but this is by no means the same phrase as the New Testament 'son of God'. 'God the Son' reflects a concern to answer the questions of Jesus' essential nature in relation to God. 'Son of God' is *primarily* much more 'functional' than this – it denotes the role of Christ as God's agent in the work of salvation.

For Paul especially, talking about what Jesus *does* seems to be prior to reflecting about what Jesus *is*. His statements about Christ are primarily soteriological (concerned with salvation). The earliest Christians were more likely to ask, 'What has Jesus done for us?' rather than,

'Does he share the divine essence?' and to ask, 'What significance does he have?' rather than, 'What substance?' This is not to deny that one question might well lead in due course to the other. However, there is (arguably) much more in Paul on the relationship with Christ of believers (who are 'in Christ' and who are 'the body of Christ'), than on the eternal relationship of Christ with God.

What I in turn had received

Reread I Corinthians 15:1–11.

What does Paul say here that he knows about Jesus, and where does he say he got it from?

One of the biggest differences, perhaps, in the faith-journey of someone like Paul and a Christian today is that Paul lived before the Gospels were written. Most Christians today will have been guided to think about things Jesus said and did, as recorded in the Gospels. The traditions and sayings that are now in the Gospels may have been circulating in various oral forms among believers, but we do not know how much of these Paul may have heard. We can make a differentiation between the early 'proclamation' (the Greek word is *kerugma* or *kerygma*) about Jesus, and the 'traditions' about what Jesus said and did.

We do not have examples of Paul's own proclamation unless 1 Corinthians 15:3–5 is a summary of what he said when he first preached in places like Corinth. The letters are not themselves proclamation of the faith, although they refer back to it (e.g. 1 Cor. 15:11) – they are pastoral teaching to those who have already heard and believed the *kerygma*. There are other indications of the early *kerygma* in passages such as Acts 5:30–2. The recurring themes are probably these: that what happened fulfils scriptural prophecies; that Jesus was crucified, buried, raised and exalted; that he died 'for our sins' or 'for us' or 'for many'; that God then sent the Spirit; that the Messiah is to return and judge; that people should repent and be baptised; and that believers should acknowledge Jesus as Lord.

By 'the traditions' about Jesus is meant the sort of material that we get in the four Gospels: narratives about Jesus' conception and birth; the baptism of Jesus; examples of his teaching, for example, the parables; healing miracles; the 'Last Supper' and how Jesus interpreted his death on that occasion; the sequence and details of passion narratives, the arrest, the trials, the words from the cross, and the narratives about the empty tomb. How much of this do we find anywhere in Paul? Did he know any of this?

There are only three explicit quotations in Paul's letters of sayings of Jesus, and they are all in 1 Corinthians.

📖   Reread 1 Corinthians 7:10.

Compare this with Mark 10:9 (and parallels: Matthew 19:6, and Luke 16:18).

📖   Reread 1 Corinthians 9:14.

Compare this with Luke 10:7 (and Matthew 10:10).

📖   Reread 1 Corinthians 11:23–5.

Compare this with Mark 14:22–5 (and Matthew 26:27–9, and Luke 22:14–20).

Where has Paul learned any sayings like these? He commends the Corinthians for maintaining **the traditions just as I handed them on to you** (1 Cor. 11:2). Of the proclamation he made to them, he says it was **what I in turn had received** (15:3). He puts it rather differently when writing about the Last Supper tradition: he says, **I received from the Lord what I also handed on to you** (11:23).

These are arguably the only three explicit citations. Are there any other echoes and adaptations of Jesus' teaching? There is a very wide range of views about this. Many readers see strong parallels in Paul's teaching in Romans 12 with sayings of Jesus in Matthew's Sermon on the Mount (Matt. 5–7), and there surely are many similarities although without close *verbal* parallels. Arnold Resch (1904) detected allusions to 925 sayings of Jesus in nine Pauline letters. This is less impressive when we discover that these include many references to *presumed* sayings of Jesus of which we have no record in the Gospels or anywhere else! On the other hand Rudolph Bultmann wrote, 'The teaching of the historical Jesus plays no role or practically none in Paul' (1976).

I received from the Lord

Paul's first contact with Christian believers, he tells us in the Letter to the Galatians, was as a persecutor of believers, zealous as he was for Jewish traditions. Then he had a revelatory encounter, a 'christophany': a vision of, or meeting with, the risen Jesus. From this he drew his vocation to proclaim the gospel; but to do so he says, 'I did not confer with any human being, nor did I go up to Jerusalem to those who were already apostles before me' (Gal. 1:16–17). It was only, he insists, after three years of this ministry that he stayed with Cephas (Peter) for a fortnight in Jerusalem, and also met Jesus' brother, James. The Book of Acts describes Paul meeting the apostles with no mention of this three-year gap, but the author of Acts is probably writing from a later perspective when some of the early, painful, differences between Paul and the church in Jerusalem were healed and in the past.

Paul himself is insistent (e.g. Gal. 1:1) that his commission to preach does not derive from the leaders of the church in Jerusalem (more of this in Chapter 5). He nowhere insists, as some readers have inferred, that all his understanding of Jesus' teaching comes out of that experience as well. He need not have known much about Jesus of Nazareth when he persecuted those who claimed he had risen from the dead: for Paul at that time, the claim that any crucified criminal was the Messiah would have seemed blasphemous. However, he was sometimes with believers from the Jerusalem church and unless they too had little value for the Jesus-traditions, it seems more than possible that some instances of them would have come Paul's way.

When Paul writes, **I received from the Lord what I also handed on to you** (11:23), he need not be (and I would argue that he is not) referring to direct revelation. He cites what must have been the liturgical tradition in the congregations he knew. Similarly, most Christians today are more familiar with the account of the Last Supper that forms part of their eucharistic worship than the versions of it in Matthew, Mark or Luke. Paul received it **from the Lord** in the sense of receiving from those who were **in the Lord** – a phrase he uses nine times in 1 Corinthians.

Imitators of Christ

Nevertheless it does seem that Paul either *did not know* the Jesus-tradition in any detail or that he *had little interest* in the Jesus-tradition (see Ziesler 1990, p. 22). This is strange for us, if we have been informed in our thinking about Christianity by any reading of the Gospels. It is not strange for Paul's pre-Gospels context. More significantly, it is not strange in terms of Paul's Christology. What did Paul need to know about Jesus of Nazareth in order for his proclamation to be effective? That he was God's Messiah, had been crucified, and had been raised by God to new life.

When Christians today consider ethical issues, they will often turn to the Gospels to see if Jesus is recorded as speaking about anything connected to the issues, or doing anything that suggests a guideline or a principle. Sometimes this is done rather naively, as if the Gospels must record Jesus' transparent and sufficient instructions on all matters of personal and political conduct. Paul does indeed refer to Jesus' teaching when he argues for a missionary's right to be supported by believers, and when he encourages married couples not to separate, but in neither case does this conclude the matter (see the discussion of Paul's own authority in Chapter 5).

He encourages imitation of Christ: **Be imitators of me, as I am of Christ** (1 Cor. 11:1). Does this imply that Paul wanted his correspondents to examine the oral traditions of Jesus' teaching and actions, such as those that later got into the Gospels, in order to model themselves closely on these? To read it like this is to detach it from its context in the letter – and this apparently happened when the text was edited into chapters, because this verse was detached from its context as the end of the argument in chapter 10 to become the start of a new section. We will examine the argument of 1 Corinthians 8–10 in more detail in Chapter 6, but for now we note that Paul wants his readers to give up and give way to other believers who are not as confident or robust in what they believe. He has illustrated how he himself gives way to others in such cases. It is *this* that he sees as imitation of Christ, and it is an imitation not of specific details of Jesus' life but of Paul's main idea about his death – that Jesus the Messiah accepted the **weakness** and **foolishness** of the cross for the sake of others. The context of this saying, and the thrust of Paul's theology, suggest that it is the pattern of the cross of Christ that is to motivate and guide believers – Paul really does **proclaim Christ crucified**.

Paul's few remarks in his letters about the character of Jesus concern his **humility** (Phil. 2:5–8) as a model for Paul's correspondents, or his **meekness and gentleness** (2 Cor. 10:1) taken as a model for Paul's own behaviour. These precisely reflect the characteristic that, Paul sees, took Jesus to the cross for the sake of others. For Paul, this is the character of Christ and therefore of Christians.

We started this chapter with the reflection that 'Christianity has a Christ who is enthroned in glory and a Jesus who washes his friends' feet'. The model of Christ as servant is central to Paul's proclamation because the cross is seen as the supreme self-subordination for the sake of others. We will need to look at Paul's eschatology (Chapter 4) to see that, in his theology, all things are then in subjection to Christ so that God may be all in all (1 Cor. 15:28).

One Lord, Jesus Christ, through whom are all things

One of the most *un*servant-like statements that Paul makes about Jesus in 1 Corinthians is where he calls him the **one Lord . . . through whom we exist**.

📖   Reread I Corinthians 8:4–6.

Does Paul contradict himself in 8:4–5? How do we resolve his monotheism with this statement about many gods?

Is there another contradiction in 8:6? How do we resolve Paul's monotheism with this statement about Jesus?

One of the fundamental statements in Jewish belief lies behind 1 Corinthians 8:6. A verse in Deuteronomy is called the *Shema* and is often recited: 'Hear O Israel: the Lord our God is one Lord' (Deut. 6:4). It is the key profession of Jewish monotheism. Jesus himself referred to it as the greatest commandment (e.g. Matt. 22:36–8). It is startling then that Paul seems to have divided up the *Shema*: **there is one God, the Father** and there is **one Lord, Jesus Christ**.

There is possibly a second formulaic statement hidden in the verse. There may have been an expression used in Stoicism (a Hellenistic school of philosophy) about the principle of unity in the cosmos: 'from whom, through whom, and for whom' all things come (Dunn 1980, p. 180). Again Paul seems to divide this principle of cosmic unity. He says that all things are **from** and **for** God, but it is Jesus Christ **through whom** we and all things exist.

This is language that the Church later made use of in Trinitarian doctrine, but the New Testament authors did not have access to these later systematic formularies, and it is difficult to see how Paul could have expected his correspondents to understand some such developed doctrine.

The most startling thing perhaps is that the verse seems to imply that Jesus had a role that went far beyond his ministry in Palestine in the 30s – a role in the creation of the world. It has parallels with a figure in Jewish thought, the Wisdom of God, personified as a woman. It was 'through wisdom' that God created all things (see Glossary item below). Is Paul saying that Jesus pre-exists the world, like the personification of Wisdom?

📁 GLOSSARY : *Wisdom, and Pre-existence Christology*

'In the beginning was the Word and the Word was with God and the Word was God . . . And the Word became flesh' (John 1:1, 14). At the end of the first century CE this New Testament text spells out the incarnation of a pre-existent Christ that the later Church reflected in its doctrine of the incarnation and its creeds.

Because this is in John's Gospel in the last decade of the first century, can we accept that the idea of a pre-existent being sent into the world from an eternal realm was assumed by Paul and his readers fifty years earlier? It is a debatable point.

What John writes of the Word ('In the beginning . . . with God . . . and the Word was God') may well reflect Jewish thought about the Wisdom of God. In Jewish thought Wisdom is with God in the founding of earth and heaven (Prov. 3.19; Wisd. 8:4–6) and she is an *hypostasis*, or personification. (It is a feminine word in both Hebrew and Greek.) It is a telling metaphor: 'Through wisdom, God created the world' means that God wisely planned and wisely acted.

While the text of John was not available for earlier writers like Paul, this idea of Wisdom as a way of talking about God was available. Paul (or one of Paul's companions) certainly uses this Wisdom language about Christ in Colossians 1. There too (as I shall argue is the case in 1 Cor. 8:6) it is a way of holding together God's purposes in creation and salvation. Because Jesus has a key role in salvation, so too he is identified with the same divine plan and power active in creation too.

Wisdom Christology provides a language for the *cosmic* significance of Christ. It raises a lot more questions – how was Jesus, an historical Palestinian of the first century, present at or before the creation of the world? John's solution of the Word, as the eternal expression of God, being made flesh, is surely unrivalled as a way of expressing the inexpressible.

However, this confirms the idea that if Paul also wanted to imply a pre-existent Christ and what we now call the doctrine of the incarnation, he would have had to explain himself (as John does) or his readers would surely not have followed his idea. He would have been taking a radically new step (Dunn 1980, p. 42).

There are other texts in Paul's letters which have traditionally been interpreted as speaking of a pre-existent Christ, as well as Colossians 1:15–20 and 1 Corinthians 8:6. These others (2 Cor. 8:9; Gal. 4:4; Phil. 2:6–11), as Dunn in particular has argued (1980, pp. 38–44, 114–23) can or should be read as referring to salvation through the cross rather than incarnation.

Christology does have a cosmic and eternal dimension, if not sometimes in pre-existence then always in a future reference. All Christology is eschatological, because God's Messiah brings in the end-time. Most christological terms refer to Christ in a *present* and *future* Lordship – usually with the resurrection of Jesus as their starting point. The final reign of Christ is in a new creation, so we will continue to discuss some of these christological questions when we turn to Paul's eschatology in the next chapter.

Remember that Paul is not producing 1 Corinthians 8:6 as a theoretical speculation or a credal summary. It is part of his teaching to the Corinthians about a practical issue about food. Food is part of God's order of *creation*, but the question is whether eating particular food is or is not significant in the order of *salvation*. Although for the Christians the pagan gods, in whose shrines animals will have been sacrificed, are not truly **gods**, they may yet be what Paul calls **demons** (1 Cor. 10:20).

Paul is seldom or never abstractly 'religious' without practical reference to the physical world. He holds together creation and salvation, and sees these two things as a unity: (i) God's plan in creation and (ii) the action of God in salvation. His (Jewish) theology of God's relationship with the world reflects the Jewish Scriptures: 'The earth is the Lord's and all that is in it, the world, and those who live in it' (Ps. 24:1). The addition, the Christian theology, is the Christology: the revelation that salvation has come through **Christ crucified**. Paul's use of the *Shema* and the Stoic formula together in one idea assert that just as salvation is *from* God *through* Christ, the same divine plan and power was and is active in creation too, from God and through Christ. (This is Dunn's argument, 1980, p. 182.)

In asserting this, Paul uses language about Christ that is used about Wisdom. Both can be identified with the creative power and action of God. Both can therefore also be spoken of as 'pre-existent' – and within the New Testament this idea is most fully expressed in John 1:1–14. It is a debatable point how far Paul speculated about the pre-existence of Jesus. What he certainly does do is to see Jesus as part of a *new* creation – we will examine this when we look at the idea of resurrection in Chapter 4 below.

Christ . . . the Wisdom of God

If we use a 'hermeneutical circle' we will not take this verse on its own but test our reading of it in the context of the whole letter and even in the context of all of Paul's writing. The glossary entry above on 'Wisdom, and Pre-existence Christology' attempts the latter very briefly. We can also examine some other references to **wisdom** in 1 Corinthians.

📖   Reread 1 Corinthians 1:20–31.

Paul uses the words **wisdom** and **wise** frequently in this passage. Perhaps some of the believers prided themselves in some way on their worldly or spiritual wisdom. If so, Paul wants them to see a great difference between God's wisdom and human wisdom. If Paul does have the Old Testament ideas about Wisdom in mind here, he is redefining it in terms of the **foolishness** of the cross.

📖   Reread 1 Corinthians 2:1–16.

This reinforces the contrast between human and God's wisdom. **Wisdom** is not here a being with God in creation but God's (wise) predetermined plan of salvation, which Jesus fulfils through his death and resurrection (2:7).

📖   Reread I Corinthians 10:1–4.

A literal reading of these verses would lead the reader to suppose that Paul believed that Christ was the rock that gave water to the Israelites in the exodus from Egypt centuries earlier. This is a figure of speech and thought called 'typology' where one thing is seen as the 'type' of another. Here God provided for the Israelites something they needed for their salvation. The life-giving rock prefigures Christ, for God has likewise provided Christ for the salvation of the people of God. The same seamless divine plan is, Paul says, evident throughout.

Philo, a Jewish author roughly contemporary with Paul, also uses typology to speak of the rock – he identifies it not with Christ but with Wisdom. This reinforces the idea that a Jew of Paul's time could readily think of Christ's role in the same way as Jewish symbolic thinking about the role of Wisdom.

Reflecting on the message and the method

Another hermeneutical circle we are wrestling with is a doctrinal one. Paul's writings were immensely influential in the formation of the later Church's theology. What Paul is forging white-hot here in his letters to the Corinthians becomes foundational for many matters of Christian belief. When we read these letters two thousand years later, it is hard to read them as if for the first time, without the Church's tradition of interpretation acting like a lens through which we read. Indeed, for many Christians it is important to be guided by their Church's doctrine in their reading of the Bible in order to understand it rightly. It was of course the purpose of the credal formularies to tell Christians what they need to know in order rightly to interpret the Bible.

The circularity here is that Paul may write, for example, **there is one Lord, Jesus Christ, through whom are all things,** and the Church after him, using insights such as these, has believed and taught a Christology where 'God the Son' has a role in creation. Today's informed reader, knowing this, is likely to assume that what the Church later derived from Paul is indeed what Paul meant and what his first readers would understand. This may be a true assumption, but it may also be a misreading. (I am not here raising a question about the Christian doctrine of Christ in creation: I am questioning whether it is necessarily the meaning Paul intended here for his first readers.)

This circle of interpretation (like that between the parts and the whole) must not be uncritical and anachronistic. While we can follow the trajectory that leads from verses in Paul to doctrines in the later Church, we cannot just reverse the trajectory and assume that the developed doctrine that the Church later expressed must be the meaning of the first indications of it in Paul. If the doctrinal tradition already expresses what Paul meant, why would we bother to read him at all if we did not think there may be new questions and fresh answers? (See, for example, the discussion in Barr 1993.)

I have suggested that 'for Paul especially, talking about what Jesus *does* seems to be prior to reflecting about what Jesus *is*.' This may help us with the paradox with which we began the chapter, that 'Christianity has a Christ who is enthroned in glory and a Jesus who washes his friends' feet'. For Paul the servanthood and Lordship of Jesus are not paradoxical at all: **Jesus Christ is Lord** (Phil. 2:11) because he **humbled himself . . . to the point of death** (Phil. 2:8). The reign of Christ is reflected in the giving up and giving way of believers (**in humility regard others as better than yourselves**, Phil. 2:3) because the reign of Christ comes about through the cross of Christ which gives the saving pattern of that humility.

The crucifixion and exaltation of the Messiah has brought about the end-times, and we must now turn to Paul's eschatological teaching.

A 'functional' Christology asks about what Jesus does in the plan of salvation. An 'ontological' Christology asks about the nature or essence of Jesus in relation to God.

✍ What do you think? Is Paul's concern with Christ ontology or function? What verses can you find in I Corinthians to support either view?

✍ Is it a false division? Does speculation on what Jesus does for humanity's salvation lead inexorably to questions of his being, his 'ontology'? What verses can you find in I Corinthians to suggest Paul makes such links?

Suggestions for further reading

Barr, J., 1993. 'Interpretation, History of: Modern Biblical Criticism', in B.M. Metzger *et al.* (eds.), *The Oxford Companion to the Bible*, Oxford, OUP, pp. 318–24

Bruce, F.F., 1980 (rev. edn). *Paul, Apostle of the Free Spirit*, Carlisle, Paternoster Press, pp. 95–125

Dunn, James, 1980. *Christology in the Making: an inquiry into the origins of the doctrine of the Incarnation*, London, SCM, pp. 163–209

Hurtado, Larry W., 1998. *One God, One Lord: early Christian devotion and ancient Jewish monotheism*, Edinburgh, T&T Clark/Continuum (reprint)

Ziesler, John, 1990 (rev. edn). *Pauline Christianity*, Oxford, OUP, pp. 24–72

In this chapter, reference was also made to the following works

Bultmann, Rudolph, 1976. *Theology of the New Testament*, vol. 1, London, SCM

Martin, Dale, 1990. *Slavery as Salvation: the metaphor of slavery in Pauline Christianity*, New Haven, YUP

Resch, Arnold, 1904. *Der Paulismus und die Logia Jesu* in A.M. Hunter, *Paul and his Predecessors*

CHAPTER 4

'All things are put in subjection': the new order

1 Corinthians 15:12—58

The place of eschatology in Paul's thinking is just as crucial for understanding his letter as the character of his Christology. The role of
Christ in the end-time is described in 1 Corinthians in terms of **subordination** or **subjection** – a key word in 1 Corinthians. This
chapter continues to investigate Paul's Christology but especially his
understanding of Christ as part of a new order of creation.

About that day or hour no one knows

There is a telling question asked and answered in another (later) New
Testament letter:

> [I]n the last days scoffers will come . . . saying, 'Where is the
> promise of his coming? For ever since our ancestors died, all
> things continue as they were from the beginning of crea-
> tion!' . . . But do not ignore this one fact, beloved, that with the
> Lord one day is like a thousand years, and a thousand years are
> like one day.' (2 Pet. 3:3—4, 8)

It seems that as unexpected decades passed after Jesus' death and
resurrection, and still the final end did not arrive, the Christians had
to defend their belief – perhaps to themselves as well – that nevertheless the final and complete reign of God was just over the horizon.

The man with a sandwich board, proclaiming 'The end is nigh' is
still a caricature of the cartoonists to indicate an *irrelevant* religious
fervour. Similarly, when the phrase 'a prophet of doom' is used, it
tends to mean a tiresome pessimist, a prophet of gloom, and the
meaning of 'Doom' as the longed-for eschatological judgement of
God is usually nowhere in the frame of meaning. Conversely, Christianity is not irrevocably associated in people's minds with a constant,

assured and hopeful expectation of the end (and transformation) of the whole created order. This might have baffled Paul.

📁   GLOSSARY : *Eschatology*

Eschaton is a Greek word that means 'last' or 'end'. Eschatology concerns the last things, the end-time.

In Judaism and the Old Testament there is a range of beliefs about the end-time. For example there is the eschatology we find in several of the prophets, involving the reign of a Messiah of David's line, and an earthly future.

Later (for example in the Book of Daniel) the hope for the future is sometimes expressed not as the agency of a Davidic king in an earthly kingdom, but through God's own intervention. This is expressed more as a heavenly, transcendent hope of a 'Kingdom of God'. In Daniel the agent of God is 'one like a human being' or 'one like a son of man' who comes 'with the clouds from heaven' and who is given everlasting dominion, glory and kingship (Dan. 7:13–14). This is sometimes described as 'apocalyptic' eschatology (*apocalypsis* means 'revelation').

It is this later strand in eschatology that also refers to the idea of resurrection (e.g. Dan. 12:2): for a discussion of resurrection, see the next section. In the inter-testamental period there was a flourishing of 'apocalyptic' and hopes for God's eschatological intervention. The book in the New Testament that most reflects this eschatology is Revelation.

There is a basic consensus in scholarship today that Jesus certainly caused an outbreak of eschatological expectation. This was by no means always accepted. The watershed was Albert Schweitzer's analysis (in the 1900s) that Jesus' teaching was thoroughly eschatological with an expectation of an *imminent* end. Dodd in the 1930s argued that the eschatological message of Jesus was a 'realised' eschatology: that is, that the end-time is to be understood as having already come in Jesus' own proclamation of the Kingdom of God. Fuller in the 1950s revised this with the phrase 'inaugurated' eschatology: that is, the end time and the Kingdom have begun but are not yet fulfilled.

The theology of the New Testament is thus based on an eschatology that we may call either realised or inaugurated. That is, the imminent expectation of the end was understood as partly fulfilled by Jesus' resurrection (the individual 'first fruits' of the final, collective Resurrection) and the receiving of the Holy Spirit. The New Age had begun, even if the Old Age had not finished.

There is consequently a tension in a lot of New Testament writing between the 'already' and the 'not yet'. How far should a believer live as if the end-times were already upon them, and how far as if the end were yet to come? The New Testament text that most thoroughly resolves this eschatological tension is perhaps the Gospel of John, which has a strongly 'realised' eschatology. In John, judgement and eternal life, and even the returned presence of Jesus (in the sending of the Spirit), are present realities and not merely future expectations for the community of that Gospel.

Some commentators suggest that elements of the Corinthian congregation expressed an 'over-realised' eschatology: that is, a conviction that they were so fully part of the new order that their spiritual condition was already unassailable.

Christ is proclaimed as raised from the dead

Paul's eschatology has features found in the eschatology of the earlier prophets, of an earthly Messiah; it also has features of the later, apocalyptic eschatology. However, the absolute key to Paul's eschatology is the factor that is not part of Old Testament eschatology: the death by crucifixion of the Messiah and his resurrection. It would be hard to overestimate the importance of this new factor in the development of Christian belief, and it did not arrive ready-packaged for the Christian Jews. There was no defined expectation in Judaism of a crucified and resurrected Messiah as the signal of the end-times. This was something the first Christians had to come to terms with and try to understand. The Old Testament texts that perhaps helped most with this understanding were the 'Songs of the Suffering Servant' in Isaiah (e.g. Isaiah 53).

For Paul initially a 'crucified Messiah' may have been the most offensive and scandalous thing about the belief of the first Christians. After the revelatory encounter he describes in Galatians, this same stumbling block seems to have become the foundation stone of his belief. It is important, in reading Paul, to recognise that he is having to forge this theology as a new thing; it does not come to him ready-made.

The concept of resurrection, however, does have a background in the Old Testament (see, e.g., Daniel 12) and in Paul's Jewish theology. It is not merely a belief that God can or will bring an individual back to life after dying. Firstly, the theology of resurrection is *corporate* rather than merely individual: it is something envisaged for the people of God: 'But at that time your people shall be delivered . . . Many of those who sleep in the dust of the earth shall awake' (Dan. 12:1–2). Secondly, the idea is not so much 'bring back to life' as 'bring to new life'. It is not resuscitation, a recovery of the life that was lost: it is a *new creative act* of God, not unlike the first creation of life, which creates a new order of life.

📖   Reread 1 Corinthians 15:12–23.

What, precisely, is it that Paul believes, which some of the Corinthians (apparently) say they do not?

📖   Read Matthew 27:50–3.

This tradition is only found in Matthew. Notice how, although Matthew recounts this as an immediate effect of the death of Jesus, he postpones the appearance of these people of God until after God raises Jesus. Compare this with what Paul says about Christ as **the first fruits**.

We saw in 1 Corinthians 15:3 that the tradition handed on by Paul **as of first importance** included the belief that Christ **was raised**. The verb is passive ('he was raised', rather than 'he rose') and here this indicates an act of God; that is, 'God raised him'. Paul reminds his correspondents of his first proclamation to them because some of them have said, **There is no resurrection of the dead** (15:12). Paul does not have to argue with them that God has raised Christ: it seems rather that some do not believe, as Paul does, that this new creative act of God is not just about Jesus, but rather signals the destiny of the created order. Paul writes a little more about what sort of life this is later in 1 Corinthians 15.

The **first fruits** is a metaphorical reference to the practice of the dedication to God of the first part of any harvest, e.g. the first sheaf reaped of a grain crop. It is a practice which is repeatedly prescribed in the Old Testament: e.g. 'You shall observe the festival of harvest, of the first fruits of your labour, of what you sow in the field . . . The choicest of the first fruits of your ground you shall bring into the house of the Lord your God' (Exod. 23:16, 19). In making this dedication, the whole of the following harvest was symbolically included.

This reflects part of Paul's theology that those who believe in Christ are 'in Christ', or are 'the Body of Christ'. If Christ has been put to death, then those who are 'in Christ' have also experienced some kind of death. If Christ has been raised, then those who are 'in Christ' must also be raised to new life. This is spelled out most clearly in another letter, Romans 6:3–11: e.g. 'if we have been united with him in a death like his, we will certainly be united with him in a resurrection like his' (v. 5). This is another instance of the eschatological tension. With the crucifixion of Christ, something has already been achieved for those 'in Christ'; the resurrection of Christ means that something more will happen. The eschatological process is inaugurated: begun but not complete.

How are the dead raised?

We are now going to jump a few verses, only to come back to them shortly. There is a second question about resurrection in 1 Corinthians 15 which it may be helpful to examine before investigating some of the other aspects of the end-time that Paul also indicates.

📖   Reread I Corinthians 15:35–44.

What contrasts does Paul draw here to describe the relationship (and difference) between physical bodies and bodies after they are 'raised'?

The second question in the chapter (15:35) is not necessarily one asked by Paul's real correspondents: Paul posits an imaginary reader who asks it because, rhetorically, the idea follows. There seem to be two key comparisons in this description of what perhaps is indescribable.

One is the continuity but difference in a **seed** that is sown with the plant that grows from it (15:36–7, 42–4). The idea of sown seeds as a symbol of life coming out of death is quite a common one in the Greek world.

The second contrast or comparison arises out of this (15:38) because different seeds produce different kind of plants. Paul expands this idea to say that different living creatures have different kinds of **flesh**; things on earth have different physical properties from things (planets and stars) in the skies, and those things in the skies differ from one another physically too. The point seems to be that we already have evidence of things which are all part of God's creation but are unlike one another. Paul is imagining that his rhetorical questioner had a limited imagination and could only think of human bodies having the physical characteristics we are familiar with. He suggests that the variety of **bodies** in God's creation points to God being capable of creating something different again in the new creation of resurrection.

Then comes the end

📖   Reread I Corinthians 15:22–8.

Paul mentions here a number of things that he believes will happen in the end-time, but he does not put them in chronological order. Can you rearrange into a time sequence all the things Paul says will happen between the resurrection of Christ and the end, when God is 'all in all'?

The resurrection of Jesus can be thought of as 'the beginning of the end'. Paul has in view an 'end of the end' which is the establishment of the final and total authority, or **Kingdom**, of God. The Church lives in the (inaugurated) end-time between the beginning-of-the-end but before the end-of-the-end.

We noted that the Old Testament offers a range of expectation about the end, including an earthly rule under a leader like David, and the transcendent rule of God. Paul finds room for both of these in a synthesis of these different eschatologies. First Jesus the Messiah will reign but a transcendent rule of God will follow at last.

One of the features of Jewish eschatological expectation is the 'woes', the trials and tribulations of the end-time (see, for example, the signs of the end that Jesus tells his followers of in Mark 13:7–20). Paul pictures these in a battle image in the circumstances of Christ's reign, when sin and death are overcome by the '**victory**' of Christ (15:55–7).

We can reconstruct the sequence of the end-time from 1 Corinthians 15 in this way:

- The beginning of the end is the resurrection (re-creation to a new life) of Christ (15:20).
- Christ comes (15:23); he is present, in this resurrection life, in the world. (This is often referred to as 'the second coming' though this phrase is not in the New Testament.)
- At this **coming**, all **who belong to him** are raised by God to the new life (15:23).
- Christ reigns (15:25) until . . .
- . . . he destroys **every ruler, and every authority and power** (15:24).
- It is in this time that the woes of the end-time are suffered.
- **The last enemy to be destroyed is death** (15:26) so that **all things are put in subjection** to Christ (15:27).
- **Then comes the end** when he **hands over** everything **to God the Father** (15:24); that is, he takes all that is subject to him and subjects this, and himself, to God (15:28).
- Then **God** will **be all in all**.

When all things are subjected

Paul lived in a social order where people were involuntarily subject to one another in interlocking social hierarchies. Slaves were subject to their owners. Women were subject to their fathers or husbands. All the people in the Empire were subject to the Roman Emperor. Whether Paul's theology challenged or supported such social inequalities will be discussed in several of the chapters in this book.

📖   Reread I Corinthians 15:27–8.

Paul achieves this extraordinary vision of the end, with language that is partly drawn from the Old Testament. Psalm 8:4–6 reads:

> what are human beings that you are mindful of them,
> mortals [literally, 'the son of man'] that you care for them?
> Yet you have made them a little lower than God,
> and crowned them with glory and honour.

You have given them dominion over the works of your hands;
you have put all things under their feet.

Compare this with I Corinthians 15:27–8.

Paul's theological world-view includes the idea of the absolute power of God. Nevertheless there are challenges to God's rule – other **rulers** and **authorities** and **powers**. Sometimes he implies that these are human agents, sometimes that they are spiritual beings and sometimes that they are more abstract concepts like 'death' and 'sin'. He calls Jesus **the Son** in the absolute in 1 Corinthians 15:28 (without any further description, such as 'Son *of God*') just as he calls God, **the Father**. By this, he possibly implies that Jesus carries out to the full the traditional relationship of a child's obedience to a parent. Jesus, unlike these opposing powers, gives God the full authority that is God's due (Delling 1972, pp. 42–3).

When the Church later formulated the creeds and debated the nature of the Trinity, there was an insistence that the Father, the Son and the Spirit were equal. Unequal models of Trinitarian relationships are sometimes referred to as 'subordinationist'. This is not the debate that Paul is engaged in here. In the Glossary entry 'Christology' in Chapter 3, I suggested that for Paul,

> . . . talking about what Jesus *does* seems to be prior to reflecting about what Jesus *is*. His statements about Christ are primarily soteriological (concerned with salvation). The earliest Christians were more likely to ask, 'What has Jesus done for us?' rather than, 'Does he share the divine essence?'

When Paul writes of the subjection or subordination of Christ to God, he almost certainly has in mind Christ as a model of humanity's service to God and to God's people, and his supreme expression of self-subjection in the crucifixion.

Paul presents a picture of Christ choosing to subject himself to God, and all other things being subject to Christ. This is a radical shift in the world order. It represents his view of the new order of the end-time. In the old order, which starts to pass away with the death and resurrection of Christ, there are many rulers and authorities and powers which subject people to their dominion. In the eschatological order, only Christ is Lord – so that in **the end**, God may be all in all.

This new order is also expressed in 1 Corinthians 8:5–6 that we examined in Chapter 3,

> Indeed, even though there may be so-called gods in heaven or on earth – as in fact there are many gods and many lords – yet for us there is one God, the Father, from whom are all things and for whom we exist, and one Lord, Jesus Christ, through whom are all things and through whom we exist.

and in other verses such as 3:23: **You belong to Christ, and Christ belongs to God**. This new order theology pervades the letter and Paul's thinking. He does not confine it to what will finally take place in the end-of-the-end but believes it has implications for behaviour, for the life of believers, as they live in the end-times.

This can be directly related to the work you have done (in Chapter 2) if you examined 1 Corinthians 2–4 for evidence that **Christ crucified** is the key idea in Paul's teaching about how believers should behave. The voluntary nature of Christian self-subordination has its pattern in the cross of Christ and its fulfilment in the final, absolute rule of God. This chapter of 1 Corinthians with its question about resurrection is not a theological parenthesis in the middle of a letter about practical matters. It is because this is Paul's christological and eschatological world-view that he applies his teaching as he does in the rest of the letter.

The last Adam

Amongst the comparisons and contrasts of physical bodies with resurrection bodies, Paul returns to the idea that Christ is the eschatological Adam. This relies on Paul's linguistic and religious identification of Adam as meaning 'humanity'. Genesis 2 and 3 provide the narrative of human nature that for Paul is representative. He can then use that story to speak about all human beings.

In another letter, to the Romans, Paul is arguing that the Jewish Law is good but not the means of salvation. He writes, 'I was once alive apart from the law, but when the commandment came, sin revived and I died . . . For sin, seizing an opportunity in the commandment, deceived me and through it killed me' (Rom. 7:9–11). This is at first sight puzzling because Paul did not live before the Law was given to Moses, and also he hadn't yet died. The puzzle can be solved with the change of one word: write in 'the serpent' instead of 'sin' at the beginning of the second sentence. 'For [the serpent], seizing an opportunity in the commandment, deceived me and through it killed me.' Suddenly it is clear (isn't it?) that the commandment is the one in Genesis 2:17, not to eat the fruit of a particular tree; and that the 'me' in the sentence does *include* Paul but is first of all the story of the first man and woman. It is Paul's story because it is all humanity's story. For Paul, to hear 'Adam' is to hear 'I' or 'we' or 'everyone' as well.

📖 Reread I Corinthians 15:21–2, 45–9.

In your head or on paper, make two lists under 'Adam' and under 'Christ' of what Paul says about each in these verses.

Note the references to human beings in these verses ('all' or 'we' or 'those who . . .'): in what ways does Paul say these are like Adam or like Christ?

Jesus is first of all like Adam – because to be a human being is to be Adam. However, starting like Adam, he doesn't end like Adam. While death came through Adam's choice (Genesis 2:17 and 3:19) the new life of resurrection comes through Christ's choice. Adam was disobedient, Christ was obedient.

The rest of humanity too starts like Adam. Because Christ has been raised and the new life has begun, the rest of humanity too can live the new life. Adam represents created humanity; Christ, new Adam, represents *re*created humanity. This idea comes here in Paul's discussion of resurrection, and his use of Adam language about Christ (sometimes called his 'Adam Christology') refers primarily to Christ risen rather than to the crucifixion or to anything in the ministry of Jesus.

Just as Paul can think of believers being 'in' Christ, so he can shift that idea to Adam, and refer to all humanity as being 'in' Adam. The phrase in 1 Corinthians 15:22, **as all die in Adam, so all will be made alive in Christ**, is one of the verses over which arguments have waged long and hard concerning whether or not Paul is 'universalist' (believing in the salvation of all people). The verse could also mean that 'all-who-are-in-Christ will be made alive' which leaves the question open. It is one feature of Paul's eschatology that he concentrates almost entirely on the destiny of the people of God, of 'the saints'. This is because these were the people to whom he was writing. We do not know what he might have said or written to those who were not 'in Christ'. It may be unhelpful for readers today to try to get answers from biblical authors like Paul to questions those writers were not trying to answer.

We will not all die

📖   Reread I Corinthians 15:50–8.

What different words does Paul use about the present and eschatological condition of those who are already dead when the end comes, and the present and eschatological condition of those who are still alive when the end comes?

Paul characterises those living as having a **mortal** body and those dead as having a **perishable** body. He envisages both as being **changed** at the coming of Christ, changed to a **body** that is **imperishable** and **immortal**: a recreation in the likeness of the risen Christ.

His use of the first person pronoun **we** in his statement, **We will not all die, but we will all be changed** (15:51) suggests that, as he writes this, Paul is envisaging the consummation of the end-times as happening within his own lifetime. There are other indications in the New Testament that its authors expected the rule of Christ as imminent. This might have been Mark's understanding when he records Jesus saying, 'there are some standing here who will not taste death until they see that the kingdom of God has come with power' (Mark 9:1). It was apparently the belief of some in the community of John's Gospel that 'the disciple Jesus loved' would not die before Jesus came (John 21:23).

📖   Reread I Corinthians 7:26–31 and 10:11–13.

Are there indications in these verses that Paul thought that the end was to come in the lifetime of believers?

📖   Reread I Corinthians 11:30.

This verse may suggest that Paul considered that for believers to be dying or to have died before the end is a sign of judgement against some of their actions. The implication is that those who act rightly will not die because they will deserve to live until the coming of Christ.

The relative dating of Paul's letters is far from certain but it may be possible to trace in Paul a *developing* eschatology. (Such developments are suggested, for example, for different reasons, by Dodd in Whiteley 1974, pp. 244ff., and Bruce 1980, pp. 309ff.) In earlier letters, Paul may believe that the coming of Christ and the general resurrection would come before he or most of his correspondents had died (so 1 Thess. 4:15, 1 Cor. 11:30; 15:51). There may have been something in the experience he calls a **sentence of death** (2 Cor. 1:9 – that we looked at in Chapter 2) that shifted him on this, because he seems then to contemplate the possibility of his own death: he writes, **if the earthly tent we live in is destroyed . . .** (2 Cor. 5:1). It is possible that the later letters after this do not reflect the same eschatological urgency as we see in, for example, 1 Corinthians 7:26–31.

This is not to say that they are *less* eschatological in their understanding of the goal of creation and the certainty of salvation – it is just the timescale that might be adjusted. As Paul says of the dead and the living, **we shall all be changed** (1 Cor. 15:51).

If the dead are not raised, let us eat and drink . . .

Some argue, though, that in the letters which reflect the more imminent expectation of the end, Paul is more negative about the physical and social world than he is in later letters.

📖 Reread 1 Corinthians 6:1–11 and then read Romans 13:1–11.

In 1 Corinthians, Paul's attitude to the civil law is apparently quite negative. The believers should not subject themselves to its judgement: the created order (and even angels are part of the order of creation) is eschatologically subordinate to those who are part of the new creation. The old order is subject to the new, under Christ.

In Romans, Paul's attitude to civil government seems much more

positive. Is this because he has different instances and circumstances in mind when he writes on two different occasions; or does
it reflect an awareness in a later letter of a period of time when the
believers must co-exist with the older order while they wait for
the end?

We saw that Paul's Christology of **Christ crucified** is not merely an
abstract, theoretical teaching but has very thorough-going practical
implications for believers. Paul's ethics involve a reversal of the usual
order of people's power, because **God chose what is weak in the
world to shame the strong** (1 Cor. 1:27). In exactly the same
way, his eschatology is not merely theoretical and, for Paul, there are
essential implications to living in the end-times. A new age has begun
in the resurrection of Christ, and a new order of social behaviour is
fitting to this new age. In his reply to those who say there is no
resurrection, Paul quotes Isaiah 22:13 (1 Cor. 15:32) to suggest that
if the eschatology he teaches is not true, then life is not more than a
few transient pleasures, and you may as well just party and die. He
may have in mind (a parody of) the Hellenistic philosophy of
Epicureanism in citing this (Thiselton 2000, p. 1253).

The connection of eschatology and ethics is signalled particularly
clearly in another letter, when Paul moves from the more theoretical
part to the ethical exhortation: 'Do not be conformed to this world,
but be transformed by the renewing of your mind' (Rom. 12:2).

The eschatological 'tension' (of a state 'already' achieved but still
'not yet' perfected) is often noticeable when Paul refers to the new
order or the end-times in his ethics. For Paul you can be at the same
time eschatologically **freed from sin** (Rom. 6:7) and yet you might
still need to be urged not to **let sin exercise dominion** (6:12) in
your life. The risen Jesus is already **Lord** for believers, but Paul calls
for a vigilance that nothing else should usurp this lordship, authority,
sovereignty in their lives.

He can even make a reference both to a 'realised' eschatology (the
condition of salvation 'already' conferred), and to the idea of the end
'not yet' come, in urging the *same* example of ethical behaviour. In
1 Corinthians 6:13–15, he is using an example of sexual immorality
in his argument about the dominion of Christ and participation in
the Body of Christ. He gives two reasons why a believer's body is
not meant for fornication. One is because the new order is already

established: **your bodies** *are* (i.e. already) **members of Christ** (6:15). The other is because God *will raise* (i.e. not yet) those same **bodies** to new life (6:14). In other words there is no *contradiction* in Paul's ethic on the grounds of the eschatological tension of the end-begun-but-not-complete, even though there is a tension over what is and what is not yet fulfilled.

Although it is something one can only deduce from Paul's response in 1 Corinthians, there is quite a consensus among commentators that some of the Corinthian believers had resolved the tension and believed that in them the fullness of the end was realised, in a sort of premature triumphalism, or an 'over-realised' eschatology. The **boasting**, the emphasis on particular charismatic gifts and the questioning that brought Paul's response of teaching about the resurrection (1 Cor. 15), may all point to this (see, e.g. Barrett 1973, p. 109; Thiselton 1978, pp. 510–26).

Reflecting on the message and the method

Different readers have read different messages from Paul's letters in terms of the implications of belief in the end on a believer's behaviour. It is widely acknowledged that he believed in a personal and spiritual transformation of a believer's life, and that this would change their individual behaviour. However, Paul has sometimes been characterised as having radical individual, personal ethics but more conservative social ethics (e.g. Gerhardsson 1982, p. 88). That is, some think that his theology did not touch the realities of the social subordinations of slave to owner, wife to husband, poor to rich.

My own opinion is that Paul's view of the social order (in the new eschatological order) was fundamentally as radical as his theology. If the 'eschatological Christology' of 1 Corinthians 15 is really at the heart of his teaching, then he believed in a world that must become subject to the authority of God in Christ. And he believed that this authority was demonstrated or achieved because of the self-subordination of Christ for the needs of the world, in the radical reversal of strength and weakness in the cross of Christ.

Because of this self-subordinating sovereignty of Christ, any other pattern of domination cannot, for Paul, be allowed to rule a believer's life. **Has Christ been divided?** (1 Cor. 1:13) he asks, outraged, when he learns that believers are claiming *other* authorities and allegiances in their lives.

In the chapters that follow, we shall be looking to see how far Paul's idea of the new order of the end-times is one in which the *final* destruction of every other **ruler and every authority and power** (15:24) is anticipated. Do women remain under the authority of their husbands, and slaves in the power of their owners, now that only Jesus is **Lord**? What of Paul's own authority as an apostle to his churches – did he hold sway over these believers by virtue of this office?

'Paul has sometimes been characterised as having radical individual, personal ethics but more conservative social ethics' (above). You may also choose to consider this statement in the light of the Christian Church today: does it operate more in personal, private behaviour, or in public, social and political life?

So far, in your reading of I Corinthians, what passages could you cite as evidence for and against a view that Christian belief makes radical changes to an individual believer but leaves the status quo of society largely unchanged?

Suggestions for further reading

Barth, Karl, 1933. *The Resurrection of the Dead*, London, Hodder and Stoughton (Eng. trans.)

Cullmann, Oscar, 1958. *The Immortality of the Soul or the Resurrection of the Dead*, London, Epworth

Fuller, R. H., 1993. 'Resurrection of Christ', in B.M. Metzger *et al.* (eds.), *The Oxford Companion to the Bible*, Oxford, OUP, pp. 647–9

Ziesler, J., 1990 (rev. edn). *Pauline Christianity*, Oxford, OUP, pp. 28–32, 73–102

Articles – e.g. 'Eschatology', 'Parousia', 'Apocalyptic', in Alan Richardson *et al.* (eds.), 1983. *A New Dictionary of Christian Theology*, London, SCM; or in B.M. Metzger *et al.*, 1993. *The Oxford Companion to the Bible*, Oxford, OUP; or in a Bible Dictionary.

In this chapter, reference was also made to the following works

Barrett, C.K., 1973. *The First Epistle to the Corinthians*, London, A and C Black

Bruce, F.F., 1980 (rev. edn), *Paul, Apostle of the Free Spirit*, Carlisle, Paternoster Press

Delling, G., 1972. 'Hupotassein', in *Theological Dictionary of the New Testament*, ed. Kittel and Friedrich, 9 vols. (1964–74) VIII, pp. 42–3

Gerhardsson, Birger, 1982. *The Ethos of the Bible*, London

Thiselton, A.C., 1978. 'Realised Eschatology at Corinth', in *New Testament Studies* 24, 510–26.

. . . 2000. *The First Epistle to the Corinthians*, Carlisle, Paternoster Press

Whiteley, D.E.H., 1974. *The Theology of St Paul*, Blackwell

CHAPTER 5

'Am I not free?': Paul's role and status with his churches

1 Corinthians 4 and 9

Paul discusses his own freedom and authority in this letter – to an extent which has led many commentators to argue that his own authority and status are among the principal issues the letter sets out to address. This chapter examines some of Paul's words about himself in the context of the surrounding sections, and attempts to relate them to the themes and theology of the whole letter.

Authority and leadership

What is the difference between someone who is authoritative and someone who is authoritarian? Does a teacher impress you more by the status they have achieved in their church or institution, or by how persuasive or effective or informative you find their teaching? Are people leaders in different spheres of life because of what they know, or because of their character or temperament, or because of some system of appointment or promotion not connected with these?

Modes of influence are complex, and our own temperaments, and experience, can be very different. For some, figures of authority deserve respect, even awe, in the first instance; for others, figures of authority in the first instance are viewed with suspicion, even hostility.

Power operates in many ways. We can use our strength to dominate others; we can use our weakness to manipulate others. Liberty is part of a person's power: how far are we free to do as we choose? Who or what is in a position to restrict our choice? Equality raises questions of relative power: are you freer than I am to do as you choose? Are some, in George Orwell's phrase, 'more equal than others' (*Animal Farm*, 1945)?

Paul's personality and theology offer a fascinating study in operations of freedom and authority. He seems to many readers to be temperamentally a fairly bossy person, yet his whole theology (if those of us are right who see **Christ crucified** as the key to it) is one of respecting the other, giving up and giving way, of insisting that his correspondents must **Judge for** [them]**selves**. As a fairly bossy person myself, I have enormous respect for his counter-temperament insistence on the essential importance of giving way. Paul's reputation among many readers and, perhaps particularly, non-readers of his letters as authoritarian, patriarchal and hierarchical, is well established but hard to square with the texts. The theologically motivated nature of Paul's understanding and exercise of authority is discussed by several commentators (e.g. Best 1986, Crafton 1991, and Schütz 1975 – who draws on Weber and Käsemann).

Though absent in body

Words of power and authority are frequent in 1 Corinthians (and also 2 Corinthians – Paul's relationship with the community continued to feature these concerns). The words are often used ironically, with a reversal of their usual meaning (we have seen this, for example, in 1 Cor. 1:25). The conflicts and disagreements which Paul seeks to reconcile are in a large measure directly about authority: who makes decisions and who has to obey, and why (Meeks 1983, p. 117).

There is a style of writing and speaking called, technically, 'diatribe', which was (and is) used by teachers to engage their audiences and draw them into the first steps of philosophic reasoning. Some commentators (e.g. Watson in Thiselton 2000, p. 791) argue that Paul's style is 'deliberative rhetoric' rather than diatribe in the strict sense, but the outcome of drawing the reader into the argument remains the same. It involves creating what is apparently a dialogue between the writer and the reader, though in fact the writer is 'playing both parts'. We have seen this several times in the passages we have looked at – for example, the questions and response Paul makes in 1 Corinthians 15:35–6, where he even calls his *hypothetical* heckler a fool! One of the features of diatribe is questions – look at any chapter in the letter and see how often they occur. Although the technicalities of rhetoric are not often discussed today, the common phrase 'a rhetorical question' is a recognition of this feature which is shared by the diatribal style. Paul uses diatribe more in these letters than anywhere else with the exception of the Letter to the Romans, where the diatribal style serves to introduce his gospel to believers he has not met (Meeks 1983, p. 122).

The intention of such a style is surely to correct but also to empower the Corinthian Christians with their own knowledge and their own access to the source of Paul's authority. The result must be that they will make independent decisions in Christian freedom, subject only to Christ.

Writing the letter is itself, however, an assertion of authority. Further, Paul makes a few explicit assertions of his own power or authority. In 5:3 Paul has **already pronounced judgement**: here they are not entirely to **Judge for** [them]**selves**. In 7:25, 7:40, he is confident that he speaks in the name of Christ.

Paul's letters are thus both 'an exercise of apostolic authority' and at the same time 'a diffusion of this authority' into his churches (Holmberg 1980, p. 186).

Servants of Christ

📖   Reread I Corinthians 3:21–4:5.

The verses at the end of chapter 3 make a summary statement of the eschatological pattern of subordination which can be compared to the one we found in I Corinthians 15:28. Try substituting 'are/is subject to' for 'belong' in 3:22 and 23.

In your head or on paper, structure this as a hierarchy with God at the top and include in their positions Christ, believers, and all the other things mentioned in I Corinthians 3:22 and 15:24–6.

Where do Paul and other Christian missionaries and pastors fit in to this structure?

Because they are 'in Christ', all creation is subject to the Corinthian believers, and no one is **leader** or ruler over them, but they are subject only to Christ. It is in this context that Paul says he wants them to think of him, not as their leader but as a **servant of Christ**. What authority, if any, does this give Paul over his congregations?

What Paul says in 4:3–5 does not seem to be about his correspondents being free from the authority of **all things**, but of Paul himself not being subject to the judgement and authority of any but God. In putting himself under God's judgement and authority here, and diminishing as **a small thing** any judgement on him of his correspondents (or anyone else), Paul implies that there is or has been a negative judgement on him from some part of the Corinthian church, and that his own authority is one part of the subject of his letter.

The language takes us back to the opening of the letter. **You belong to Christ**, is Paul's answer to whatever was dividing the believers in Corinth (1:10–12), making some of them say or imply **I belong to Paul**. (The Greek text does not use a word for 'belong to' in either place but uses the same grammatical form in each: 'I am of Paul', 'You are of Christ', etc.) All four of the opening chapters focus on this issue. Throughout them, Paul insists that nothing and no one can have sovereignty in their lives other than Christ. Whatever authority Paul has with them must not obscure that.

He has used a number of metaphors to describe the fundamental relationship of the believers with Christ and with Paul. He says that they are God's field, and that Paul planted, Apollos watered, but that it is God who gives the growth (3:6–9). He says that they are God's temple, that Paul is a master builder who has laid the foundation, the foundation is Christ, and others have built on the foundations (with the possibility that some have built well, some badly) (3:10–16). The recurring word in the NRSV and several other translations describing Paul's role is **servant** and this reflects the Greek word for servants (*diakonoi*) in 3:5, but in 3:9 it translates 'co-workers' (*sunergoi*), and in 4:1 a word (*huperetēs*) which in other Greek texts can cover a range of assistants and subordinates.

The predominance of words for servant and service in the roles that Paul sees people taking in the church, coupled with the key pattern of Christ's subordination and self-offering, makes for a mutuality, a reciprocity, in the relations of believers with those who proclaim, teach, lead or build. Paul does urge his correspondents to offer service to certain people in the church, but their qualifications for receiving any such service is that they themselves are *serving* the believers: see for example 1 Corinthians 16:15–16.

Paul consistently insists that whatever authority he has is his because it is delegated by God. This could still lead him to claim considerable authority over the Corinthians so that it would not be unreasonable for them to have said, **I belong to Paul**. However, to do this is to remain at what Paul calls the (merely) **human** level rather than being **spiritual people** (3:1–4). Paul repeatedly reminds them that they have direct access – not merely through his agency – to the source of his own and all authority: **God's Spirit dwells in you** (3:16); **All things are yours** (3:21).

Learn through us

Nevertheless, his role, and consequently his authority, is an issue between them. Paul's treatment of the issue shows that for him it is theological and universal – not merely a matter of his own personal temperament or style.

📖   Reread 1 Corinthians 4:6–13.

What implications can we draw from 4:6–7 of the attitude or behaviour of (some of) the Corinthian Christians? Does it match the implications of any other part of 1 Corinthians?

In 4:10, Paul says, **We are weak but you are strong**. Is there an echo of 1:27 here and if so, what is Paul's point?

Paul's claim in 4:6 to **have applied all this** to Apollos and himself for his correspondents' benefit puts the spotlight back on to them and their behaviour. The factionalism and spiritual pride that seems to be in the community challenges Paul's role and relationship with them. However, he does not want merely to defend his own role and relationship but to bring them to an understanding and behaviour that responds to the gospel he has brought them. However much Paul minds about how they view him – and he clearly does – he minds more about their response to Christ crucified. The rhetoric of his question (4:7) contrasts **boast** with **gift**: he presents to them a picture of those who take pride in their spiritual status as if it were their own achievement rather than something offered freely to them. The picture is the stronger for his previous words about the cross and about those to whom this offer was made: **God chose what is low and despised in the world** (1:28).

His exhortation to **learn through us** (4:6) is worth tracing through the letter. Paul often avoids writing, 'Do this' in favour of phrases which refer to what he himself chooses or prefers to do. See, for example, how the **you** in 8:12 shifts to **I** in 8:13. Far from standing above his converts, he allows them to see his own vulnerability to failure – and the irony that in saving others he might still be **disqualified** (9:27). Paul is only *worth* imitating in so far as he imitates Christ (11:1) and Christ was crucified.

He refers once more to **Apollos** after this passage – see 16:12. There is an open acknowledgement here that Paul has no authority over this fellow-worker: Paul's wishes were overruled by Apollos' own decision. This is one of several disclaimers of power in the letter.

In 4:8 Paul effectively parodies the boasts of those believers whose 'over-realised' eschatology leads them (apparently) to proud claims of spiritual riches. There is a similar reproach to another church from a slightly later New Testament writer – 'you say, "I am rich, I have prospered, and I need nothing." You do not realize that you are wretched, pitiable, poor, blind, and naked' (Rev. 3:17).

His characterisation of himself is partly a metaphor about being like a convict sentenced to be killed in the gladiatorial games, and partly autobiographical description. Such a catalogue of sufferings is a rhetorical device with parallels in other Greek literature (Fitzgerald in Thiselton 2000, p. 360). Paul surely sees them as linked both with the pattern of Christ crucified and with the woes of the end-times. If the expressions seem at all exaggerated (especially to our modern minds, unused to this sort of rhetoric) we should probably remember that Paul is contrasting his being treated as **rubbish** to some Corinthians believing themselves to be **kings**. If one statement is 'over the top', perhaps it is meant to show up the other exaggerated claim (Thiselton 2000, p. 360).

My beloved children

📖 Reread I Corinthians 4:14–21.

What does this passage suggest to you about the relationship that Paul believes he has with these people, and their perceptions of him?

We saw in his letter to Philemon that Paul uses the metaphor of fatherhood in relation to those he has brought to faith in Christ. In

Philemon there was no sense of **father** as an authority figure. Here Paul does include the admonishing, authoritarian parental role in his relationship with them (4:14) and alludes to two possibilities in parent-child relations: that he could come **with a stick, or with love in a spirit of gentleness** (4:21). The **stick** at least is clearly metaphorical, and the rhetoric points to their obvious preference for the loving gentleness of Paul as their **father**. He has used the metaphor of parental relations earlier in the letter in 3:2. There the metaphor seems closer to the role of a nursing mother than of any kind of authority figure, and moreover is a picture of a *temporary* expedient: the end even of that nurturing relationship is that the Corinthians will mature beyond the need for it.

While Paul is actually not in a position to punish them – even were he so minded – he is in a position to make them ashamed. This is a claim to the authority of one who knows better than they, and in a position to point out their waywardness. Even this he says he is not doing (4:14), though the very statement **I am not writing this to make you ashamed** could be intended to induce such shame – and this too is a common rhetorical device. He contrasts his role with other potential **guardians** they might have in Christian life. This metaphor is based on the role of a *paidagōgus*, a slave or servant who would supervise and correct a child. Paul therefore *contrasts* his role with those who merely supervise and correct, those who in effect merely **come with a stick**.

The idea of imitation of Paul is again raised here (4:16–17). Instead of imitating Paul, some of the Corinthians have been **arrogant** (4:19) – the same surely of whom Paul says, **Quite apart from us you have become kings!** (4:8). Imitation of Paul, therefore, must reflect what he has described of himself in 4:10–12: they too should be **weak** and **fools for the sake of Christ** (4:10). Again, Paul declares that he is only worth imitating if his life is patterned after Christ crucified.

Am I not an apostle?

The other place in the letter where Paul turns the spotlight in a sustained way on himself is in 1 Corinthians 9. Many commentators have seen the section as a defence of Paul's authority and apostleship as if this were his main concern and the primary issue to be addressed. As

such they have seen it as something of a parenthesis, even an interpolation, in a part of the letter where Paul is encouraging them in
certain behaviour about eating food (or not) which has been offered
to pagan deities. When we look at the argument of 1 Corinthians 8
and 10 (in the next chapter), we will see how thoroughly 1 Corinthians 9 addresses the argument Paul makes there of the strong
giving way to the weak after the pattern of Christ crucified. As in
other places in the letter he urges an imitation of his practice, not as
an assertion of his authority but as an example of how the theology
and ethics of 'Christ crucified' is to be applied in their lives.

📖   Reread 1 Corinthians 9:1–2.

**What might we construe about Paul's view of apostleship from
verse 2?**

There is an echo here of the idea in 4:15, **though you might have
ten thousand guardians in Christ, you do not have many
fathers**. His claim to be listened to by the Corinthian believers is
because they came to faith through his proclamation. His authority is
based on his special relationship with the community. The theology of
the reversal of weakness and power means that his role is no less
effective for being **least of the apostles, unfit to be called an
apostle** (15:9).

🗀   GLOSSARY : *Apostle*

The Greek word *apostolos* means
'one who has been sent'. Christian
use has defined it in a particular
way – it does not occur often in
other Greek texts of the period
(Betz in Metzger 1993, p. 41).

The verb *apostollein* has a similar
range of meaning to that of 'to send'
in English. If someone is sent, they
might be merely the bearer of a
message, with no authority apart
from that of the words of the
sender in the message. On the

other hand, it is also possible to
send someone on your behalf and
give them authority to act for you,
as your representative or delegate,
like an ambassador acting and
speaking for a nation's president or
sovereign. Which end of this
spectrum is 'apostle' in the New
Testament?

It is clear from Acts 1:21–6 that
Luke uses the world 'apostle' for
the twelve named disciples accom-
panying Jesus in his ministry. When

he writes of the congregation in Jerusalem wanting to replace Judas with a twelfth person, he shows them appointing a man (the possibility of a woman fulfilling the role is not raised) who accompanied Jesus from his baptism to his ascension: crucially, one who can give witness to the resurrection. For Luke, 'apostle' is a delegate of Christ with distinctive and primary authority in the church.

It is possible that there was a contention among the earliest churches about who could claim the title of apostle, and, if they did, what authority they had. John's Gospel avoids the word 'apostle' entirely, though it has many references to Jesus 'sending' his disciples and friends just as the Father 'sent' him. John refers to the twelve disciples merely as 'the Twelve'.

There was surely a dispute about how far Paul could have the title or role of apostle: he writes, 'If I am not an apostle to others, at least I am to you' (1 Cor. 9:2), and always asserts the title in opening a letter.

Paul does not subscribe to the use that reserved the term only for those who had accompanied Jesus from baptism to resurrection. Like John he refers to these as 'the twelve' (1 Cor. 15:5). He does use the term of the leaders of the Jerusalem church, including James the brother of Jesus (Gal. 1:19). He may be conscious of the Lukan criteria: when he refers to himself as an apostle, one thing he refers to is that he too is one who has 'seen Jesus our Lord' (1 Cor. 9:1).

The second criterion he appeals to is functional: 'Are you not my work in the Lord?' (1 Cor. 9:1). It seems to me characteristic of Paul to appeal primarily on the basis of what you *do* rather than what you *are*. (We can compare this with the functional emphasis in his Christology.) The argument, for Paul, is that whatever authority is or is not attributed to him by others, he must have been delegated with authority from God because he has 'won' people for Christ. 'You will know them by their fruits,' he could have said, if he had had the opportunity of reading Matthew 7:16.

Paul therefore uses the term for others who are missionaries such as Andronicus and Junia, 'prominent among the apostles' (Rom. 16:7). As such, women as well as men have the name, because they perform the function.

We will discuss in Chapter 8 how far Paul gives pre-eminence to apostles, or any other, among the functions or roles of members of churches.

We have not made use of this right

📖   Reread I Corinthians 9:3–14.

What reasons and authorities does Paul give (there are several) for the practice of missionaries or apostles (and their spouses) being supported by their congregations?

What is the one reason Paul gives for choosing not to do so himself?

Paul mentions the practice of **Cephas** (Peter), **the brothers of the Lord** and the other **apostles**. It seems very likely that the Jerusalem-based churches led by Peter and James supported their pastors and missionaries. If they were a collection of congregations amounting to some few thousands of people, located principally within Judea and Galilee, this would not have been impossible economically, even among the poor (Goulder 1994). However, Paul's missionary practice meant that he travelled great distances between house-churches of perhaps fifty members or fewer with whom he would then have needed to stay for weeks or months at a time – an entirely different economic proposition except for the very affluent.

Paul's differences from the leaders of the Jerusalem church seem to have been a site of contention in the early decades of Christianity. Here Paul argues that he has as much right as such leaders to be supported but that he chooses not to be so. Why does he need to protest this? It seems likely that the support received by some missionaries or leaders was perceived as an explicit indication of their authority in those communities. The fact that Paul was not supported by his congregations, may have appeared to some to indicate that he could claim no such authority among them.

In 9:14 he claims the authority of words of Jesus to the practice of supporting missionaries (a tradition recorded later in Luke 10:7 and Matt. 10:10). We noted in Chapter 3 that there are few explicit citations of Jesus' words in Paul's letters (though some argue for allusions to several or many). It is perhaps extraordinary that this is one of very few explicit sayings of Jesus cited by Paul, and he *does not carry out* the practice commanded in it. He does not practise what Jesus commands. He does not *challenge* it – on the contrary he insists on the right to do it as commanded by Jesus. However, he also claims the right to put the theology of **Christ crucified** into practice in a way that does not reflect this command of Jesus.

Something similar is evident in 1 Corinthians 7:25 where he writes on a subject about which he has **no command of the Lord**, but he nevertheless goes on to give his **opinion as one who by the Lord's mercy is trustworthy**. Paul distinguishes between a **command of the Lord** and his own opinion, but he is not dependent on commands of the Lord, sayings of Jesus, in order to make decisions and teach others. He may even, as in 9:14, choose to do something other than what **the Lord commanded**. Authority in Christ may be drawn from something other than the tradition. Paul, and other believers, may themselves be **trustworthy, by the Lord's mercy**. This is all of a piece with Paul's exhortation to **be imitators of me as I am of Christ** (11:1). It is conforming to the wisdom of God revealed in **Christ crucified** that guides the believer, and **these things God has revealed to us through the Spirit** (2:10).

A slave to all

📖 Reread I Corinthians 9:15–27.

Elsewhere Paul reproves believers for **boasting** about anything concerned with the gospel and their spiritual condition. What, if anything, is different about his ground for boasting here?

There is a convoluted argument in 9:15–18, and Paul is passionate about it – he says, **no one will deprive me of my ground for boasting**! He believes that his apostleship, the vocation to proclaim the gospel of Christ, is a commission given to him by God. Because it is from God and not something he has chosen for himself, he is not to be commended for undertaking the role – whether he undertakes it willingly or unwillingly. This is a fascinating insight into Paul's spirituality – both his character and his theology. His theology is fundamentally one of grace: salvation and all the blessings of God are free gift: not earned, not merited, but given. To respond to the gospel is not to offer anything in return but merely to receive the gift. He wants to do more than is required of him, to offer something beyond accepting the gift of God.

He has reproved the Corinthians (or some of them) for some sort of spiritual pride reminding them that what they have received is through the grace of God: **God chose what is low and despised in the world . . . so that no one might boast in the presence of God** (1:28–9). Their claims to be spiritually powerful, spiritually rich, are apparently being made in some way that they are boasting about themselves rather than **in the Lord** (1:31). Paul's **ground for boasting** is not that he has put himself higher than others but that he has not put himself as high even as he might by his **rights in the gospel**, rather lower, with **the dregs of all things** (4:13). He has chosen something that does not deny the free gift of the gospel by claiming to be worthy of it with a spiritual status; rather he has chosen something to offer which reflects the gift of grace: **I may make the gospel free of charge**.

This is all of a piece with what he has said about his role, one who is serving and not served (3;5, 9; 4:1), a parent who guides by example rather than correction (4:15–17), one who is bold enough to command but would rather appeal on the basis of love (Philem. 8–9).

For the paradox of 'freedom' in Christ and becoming 'a slave' of Christ and of others, see Chapter 10.

The Corinthians are not subject to Paul's own authority: rather both are subject to **Christ's law** (not explained here but effectively the command to love). Paul even concedes the theoretical possibility of the Corinthians succeeding where he fails: **so that after proclaiming to others I myself should not be disqualified** (9:27).

Reflecting on the message and the method

In his letter to Philemon, Paul wrote, **though I am bold enough in Christ to command you to do your duty, yet I would rather appeal to you on the basis of love** (Philem. 8–9). So in this letter, arguably, Paul demonstrates the same boldness but also the same preference for the 'weakness' or vulnerability of love.

Any good teacher offers students the ability not to remain in subordinate pupilhood but to develop the understanding and skills to operate with the same authority as their teacher. Paul explicitly discusses the sources and limits of his authority with his congregation in 1 Corinthians. He believes that they have the same access to spiritual authority as he does. His is a 'dialectical authority' (Jaubert in Holmberg 1980, p. 119) that enables his correspondents to receive his authority and to develop their own. The result of his letter in part at least is to help readers make independent decisions in Christian freedom.

One consequence of the inclusion of these letters in the canon of the New Testament is that 'the authority of Scripture' attaches to them for Christians today. This sets up a tension (not necessarily a contradiction) between the authority which this accords the text of 1 Corinthians and the limitations Paul sets to his authority in the letter (and additionally a tension with the authority it may or may not have had for the Corinthian believers). More of this in the final chapter.

✏ At this stage, how far do you find Paul's strategies of influence coercive and authoritarian? How far are they in keeping with a theology of *voluntary* and *mutual* subordination?

Suggestions for further reading

Bennett, David W., 1993. *Metaphors of Ministry: biblical images for leaders and followers*, Carlisle, Paternoster Press

Best, Ernest, 1986. 'Paul's Apostolic Ministry', *Journal for the Study of the New Testament*, 27, pp. 3–25

Betz, Otto, 1993. 'Apostle', in B.M. Metzger *et al.* (eds.), *The Oxford Companion to the Bible*, Oxford, OUP, pp. 41f.

Crafton, J.A., 1991. *The Agency of the Apostle*, Sheffield, JSNT Supplement Series, pp. 53–103

Elliott, N., 1994. *Liberating Paul: the justice of God and the politics of the apostle*, Sheffield, Sheffield Academic Press

Stott, John, 2002. *Calling Christian Leaders: biblical models of church, gospel and ministry*, Leicester, IVP

In this chapter, reference was also made to the following works

Goulder, M., 1994. *A Tale of Two Missions*, London, SCM

Holmberg, B., 1978. *Paul and Power: the structure of authority in the primitive church as reflected in the Pauline epistles*, Uppsala, CWK Gleerup

Meeks, W., 1983. *The First Urban Christians*, Yale, YUP

Schütz, J.H., 1975. *The Anatomy of Apostolic Authority*, Cambridge, SNTS Monograph Series

Thiselton, A.C., 2000. *First Epistle to the Corinthians*, Carlisle, Paternoster Press

CHAPTER 6

'This liberty of yours': questions of social status

1 Corinthians 8 and 11:17–34

Two of the issues that Paul addresses in 1 Corinthians are almost certainly related to the financial circumstances of some of the people involved. These passages give us the opportunity to see how Paul relates his theology of following the pattern of Christ crucified to a community where some people are richer than others. Does his teaching support or subvert the social system of giving higher status to those of greater wealth? If all Christians are to be subordinate to one another's needs, are some (to adapt Orwell's phrase) to be *more subordinate* than others?

Social status

What gives a person greater respect or power in our society? Older hierarchies of social class do not structure people's behaviour or opportunities in Britain to anything like the extent they once did. However, property, income, job, education and other social circumstances may, variously, have an effect on everyone's choices of lifestyle, and on the way some people treat some other people. If we are trying to cross a road in a hurry and find our way impeded by someone, do we give way with more, or less, grace to a chauffeur-driven stretch-limousine or a homeless person pushing a supermarket-trolley? Are we conscious when we do of our power or status in relation to either?

In any society that uses money or trade-tokens, of course, richer people have more choices, whether or not they are treated with greater esteem.

When you come together

The social patterns and entrepreneurial culture in Roman Corinth may have encouraged strong elements of status-consciousness (Witherington 1995, p. 21). A Pauline congregation seems to have generally reflected a fair cross section of urban society (Meeks 1983, pp. 51ff., 72–3). The extremes, top and bottom, of the Greco-Roman social scale may not have been represented, but the Corinthian church was a congregation in which people of several social levels were brought together. This was not unprecedented: a number of other organisations brought together a cross section of society, but the Christian communities may have brought together a wider range than most. More significantly, they may have brought them together with an expectation of some equality between the members.

Within the larger society of the Greco-Roman world, the Christian movement was what social-scientists call a 'conflict' movement because it was in tension with some of the hierarchical institutions of that society (such as slavery and the patriarchal family – more of both of these in later chapters). The Christian community did not withdraw from the rest of society as did other communities where some institutions of dominance were rejected and women admitted in full membership (Fiorenza cites the Epicurean Garden and the Jewish Therapeutae: 1983, p. 214). Nor, apparently, did Christians mount a social and political challenge (how could they?) to these institutions and hierarchies. Therefore, free people, freed people and slaves were admitted to the Christian movement while they still continued to live with pagan spouses or in pagan households. Paul's exhortations testify to the tensions between the alternative Christian community and the larger society. In the community there may have been certain freedoms and expectations of equality, which did not exist when the community was not assembled.

Further, there were individuals and groups, within those levels, who would have experienced what social scientists call high 'status-inconsistency' or 'status-dissonance' (Meeks 1983, p. 22; Witherington 1995, p. 23), that is, they ranked high according to some status indicators, like wealth, but low in others, like occupational prestige. The significance of this is that there were likely to be conflicts or differences of perception not only between persons but also between different kinds of authority (Meeks 1983, p. 122). The role of the householder with a house large enough to accommodate the congregation presents one instance: was he or she a patron, a host, a provider of food, a leader of that congregation? Would s/he be expected to take a different role in the gathering of Christians from those other occasions when, for example, business associates might be invited to a feast?

'Brothers and sisters' the members may have been when assembled, but when the social circumstances of their secular lives made differences between their behaviour, was any of them meant to compromise their social behaviour?

Now concerning food sacrificed to idols

📖   Reread 1 Corinthians 8:1–6.

Now concerning . . . may be a phrase Paul uses when he addresses in turn a number of issues raised – perhaps in a letter from the Corinthian believers – see 7:1. Can you reconstruct their possible question from the beginning of Paul's response here?

It is particularly evident here that we are hearing only one side of a conversation. We are plunged into a debate where **the eating of food offered to idols** and claims to **possess knowledge** are significant.

🗁   GLOSSARY : *Hellenistic religion*

Judaism and Christianity are monotheistic, holding the belief that there is one God. Most of the populace of the Roman Empire were polytheistic in their practices. There were many gods and goddesses and lesser divinities and many shrines and temples to them, with priesthoods and sacrifices.

The God of Judaism is a trans-cendent creator 'from whom are all things and for whom we exist' (1 Cor. 8:6). There are other spiritual agencies sometimes mentioned in Judeo-Christian texts – such as angels and demons – but these are created beings and not themselves gods. In Hellenistic religion, human beings and gods are not always absolutely distinct. Gods may be mistaken for human beings (like

Paul and Barnabas being taken as Zeus and Hermes in Acts 14) and human beings may become 'divine' (Caesar in 48 BCE was decreed 'the god on earth and universal saviour of human life').

Much of the meat that was eaten in a place like Corinth would have been slaughtered at a god's shrine as a sacrificial offering. Part may have been burnt on an altar. Part may have gone to the priests or priestesses of the shrine. The rest could then be sold in the market place to anyone who could afford meat for a meal.

The Jews kept a week of seven days with the seventh day as a day of rest. There was no such weekend holiday in the Roman calendar. Holidays or holy days occurred irregularly as a scattering of feasts and festivals throughout the year, not a weekly Sabbath. Feasts and festivals were held on these days with sacrifices. (Paul's metaphor of running a race in 1 Corinthians 9:24 may refer to the local festival of the Isthmus games of Corinth – the athletic games too were an offering to a god.)

On these and other such days, a feast might be hosted in the shrine or temple of a god. Here the guests would participate in eating meat offered at the shrine in a cultic meal as part of the festival (Theissen 1982, p. 128; Meeks 1983, p. 69).

There are of course many other aspects to Hellenistic religion(s). The rudiments sketched above may serve to give a background to the practices referred to in 1 Corinthians 8 and 10.

📁 GLOSSARY : *Gnosticism*

There are several second-century texts by individuals or groups, some of whom call themselves 'Gnostics', that refer to a special knowledge (Greek, *gnōsis*). While these movements must have developed to some extent during the New Testament period, none of the documents is as early as this; therefore it is hard to know of what, if any, forms of these gnostic or gnosticising movements Paul may have been aware.

Some beliefs of the later movements include the following:

(a) the true nature of the world and the believer's condition constitutes a saving knowledge (*gnōsis*);

(b) the world is the creation of a 'demiurge', a lesser god than the true transcendent God, and material things are not good; the spiritual self, the soul, is trapped in the material body and must escape from it;

(c) there is a divine spark in humanity which is the true spiritual self, imprisoned in matter; in this way humans are, or can be, like the divine.

In the second century the Church Fathers wrote against these movements and these ideas. It is clear that they do not conform to Christian and Jewish theology, where it is the one true God who creates the material world and sees that it is good (Gen. 1:31). Human beings in Judeo-Christian thought are not good spirits trapped in bad bodies (though the history of Christian thought has sometimes reflected such an idea) but selves which are both flesh and spirit, and the destiny of this whole self is to be transformed in God's act of resurrection.

The rejection of the material world could lead either (and mostly) to asceticism, where believers abstained from food and sex and material possessions. It might also lead to permissive ethics: if the material world is worthless and the creation of a rejected divinity, it might be thought that physical indulgence is not significant or even that the creator's laws should not be obeyed (Wilson 1993, p. 256).

How far these ideas originated in Jewish, Greek, Egyptian or Asian thought is disputed by scholars today. How far the Christians of the New Testament period were influencing or being influenced by them is hard to assess. Late in the first century, a Pauline Christian writes, 'Avoid the . . . contradictions of what is falsely called knowledge [gnōsis]' (1 Tim. 6:20). Earlier, Paul quite often uses the word: in any theology there must be a true knowledge as well as a 'false' knowledge. However, he may or may not have the gnōsis of the Gnostic (or pre-gnostic) groups in mind when he uses the word.

Paul uses the word often in 1 Corinthians: here it is mostly positive and seems not to refer to the Gnostics' type of knowledge. For example, he gives thanks that the believers in Corinth have been enriched in Christ 'in speech and knowledge of every kind' (1:5).

Do some of the Corinthians use the word to mean a special saving knowledge such as the Gnostics later taught, and is Paul aware of this? Most of the times he uses it are in 1 Corinthians 8, where he is evaluating 'knowledge' positively (agreeing with them that 'all of us possess knowledge') but not as the highest principle, because 'Knowledge puffs up, but love builds up' (8:1–2).

If the Corinthians were applying a gnostic tendency to their belief in Christ, this would lead them to hold that eating meat offered at pagan shrines was not significant (reflecting the permissive ethics that the material world carries no spiritual value). However, Paul seems to expect them to agree that there is one God who has created the world 'and its fullness' and that this is the ground of their true knowledge (8:6; 10:26). There seem to be no signs that he is combating a 'false' knowledge.

It may be helpful to bear in mind when reading Paul's letters that some of his correspondents may have tendencies either to asceticism, or to libertinism (both can stem from rejections of the spiritual value of the material world) even if such tendencies seem unlikely to be expressions of any-

thing like full-blown Gnosticism. played some part in the thought-
Some of the ideas that are taken up world of some of the people in
in those later movements may have Corinth and elsewhere.

The nature of the **knowledge** of which Paul speaks, and which is
somehow ranged against the claims of **love**, becomes clearer in the
next verses.

(For a discussion of 1 Corinthians 8:4–6, see chapter 3.)

This liberty of yours

📖 Reread 1 Corinthians 8:7–13.

What, according to Paul, are the reasons why it is right to eat meat
offered to idols, and what are the reasons why it might be wrong?

Paul is dealing with Christians who differ and he seems concerned for
both groups. However, he directs his reply to one group of them, and
to a large extent identifies with them. On one side there are those he
implies are the **strong** (cf. Rom. 15:1), and these possess a certain
knowledge (8:4, 10) and therefore insist upon their **freedom**
(8:9; 9:1; 10:29) and **right** (9:4ff.; 10:23f.). On the other side,
there are those he calls the **weak** (8:9; 9:22) with **weak consciences** (8:7, 12) – for whom the eating of sacrificed meat is a very
serious, indeed a dangerous, matter (8:7). **Conscience** is here effectively consciousness (or knowledge) of what is right or wrong.

In Corinth, because of social differences, a believer's perception of
what it meant to eat meat would have been likely to be different
depending on whether s/he were rich or poor. The poor rarely had
meat. Their diet would have been largely or exclusively vegetarian,
because this was cheaper. When they did eat meat, it was often as part
of pagan religious celebrations (Theissen 1982, p. 128). For example,
there was sometimes a public distribution of meat for a ceremonial
religious occasion; most community celebrations were also religious
feasts. For this reason, eating meat and worshipping idols would have
been closely associated in the experience of the poor.

It was otherwise for the richer or more socially powerful of the
believers for whom meat formed a larger part of their routine diet –

meat bought in the market place but which may well have been from an animal offered at a pagan shrine. Moreover, if they did not buy such meat for their own households, these would have been people who might accept invitations to dinner where meat would be served because of social or business obligations.

Paul's teaching takes account of both parties: 'the wishes (or prejudices) of the weak are upheld, and so is the knowledge (and social privilege) of the strong' (Theissen 1982, p. 139). At the same time the teaching is based on a principle that cannot be compromised. If there are those who are being adversely affected by whether or not fellow-believers eat meat (because they associate it with idol-worship) they must be seen, whatever their social or financial status, as brothers or sisters **for whom Christ died**. That is their status among believers, and there is no status higher.

Note that those who are to give way are the people who, like Paul, are clear or confident in their consciences that the idols are not truly gods, and that all things come from the one God whom they worship (8:6). They have the 'stronger', more robust faith, and are likely to have a higher social, financial status. It seems that it was some of this group who had written, **all of us possess knowledge** (8:1), which Paul is probably quoting back at them here. Paul agrees in principle: this is their common faith. Yet in fact not all the believers are secure in this knowledge. This does not stop them being brothers and sisters, and those for whom Christ died. To insist on your rights and freedom – even those conferred on you by faith in Christ – is to be puffed up with knowledge rather than to be built up, with others, by love (8:1). Being 'built up' is a corporate idea, not an individualistic one (see Chapter 8 on 'the Body of Christ', and the Glossary item 'Koinōnia' in Chapter 1).

Notice in 8:13 that Paul does not make a judgement on their practice in terms of an imperative, an order of what to do. He phrases his exhortation as a statement about his own choices in such a situation. (Remember his stated preference in Philemon 8–9.) The whole of 1 Corinthians 9 then follows as a key illustration of this principle – that although you may have rights and freedoms in your faith in Christ, the pattern of God's grace and of Christ crucified is a call to giving way to the needs of others: 'For though I am free with respect to all, I have made myself a slave to all' (9:19).

Eating in the temple of an idol

In 1 Corinthians 8, eating consecrated meat at a private meal is countenanced in principle; what is not countenanced is disturbing a **weak** person by doing so. The debate seems to shift when Paul returns to the issue in 1 Corinthians 10.

📖 Reread 1 Corinthians 10:1–22.

What, here, are Paul's reasons for not eating food offered at a pagan shrine?

Paul uses the Exodus story of the people of Israel (Exod. 32) as an example to teach the Corinthians to **flee from the worship of idols** (10:14). The teaching is still that idols are not gods, or even **anything** (10:19, cf. 8:4), but that because pagans sacrifice to **demons** and not to God (10:20, cf. 10:5) to eat such food is a sharing in the **table of demons** (10:21).

It is likely that Paul is addressing (at least) two different types of occasion. In 1 Corinthians 8 (except for v. 10) the occasion in mind is probably in a private household – either buying meat in the market for the Christian's own household or where a Christian has been invited to a meal in a pagan household. Here it is not wrong to eat meat offered to idols if no weak fellow-Christian is offended when you do. In 1 Corinthians 10:1–22, Paul seems to have a different occasion in mind: one that he had referred to briefly – as an extreme example perhaps – in 8:10, **eating in the temple of an idol**. What Christians cannot do, however confident and robust their faith and conscience, is to participate in a cultic meal that is held in the shrine of a pagan deity, which clients of a non-Christian patron might be invited to do (Meeks 1983, p. 69).

Even on this matter, Paul refers them to their own judgement, and not to his: **Judge for yourselves** (10:15).

Do not seek your own advantage but that of the other

📖 Reread 1 Corinthians 10:23–11:1.

Paul implies that his liberty is *not* 'subject to the judgement of someone else's conscience' (10:29). To what then is it subject?

Paul reverts to the first two occasions he had in mind, those of buying meat in the market themselves (10:25), and the private meal in a pagan household (10:27). He does two things which many a good teacher will do – he summarises the principle of what he has been discussing (10:23) and gives an illustration to apply the principle (10:28ff.).

His summary seems again to use one of the Corinthians' own phrases: **All things are lawful** (also in 6:12; cf. 8:1). This is teaching they may have derived first of all from Paul himself in his first proclamation to them. So Paul could be quoting the Corinthians who were quoting him. This would suggest that some at least of the Corinthians' questions in their letter (7:1) concerned further explanation of Paul's own teaching to them, rather than (as commentators have sometimes argued) new introductions of issues foreign to Paul's gospel.

The Greek word translated in the NRSV as **are lawful** is *exestin*, and this verb and related words like *exousia* are used several times in this letter. *Exousia* is the word Paul uses for authority from God – it conveys power, rights, freedom. It would be quite in character for Paul to have taught his congregations that through the gospel **all things** were **lawful** for them, for they are now subject only to Christ. He says the same in 6:12, and follows it with 'I will not be dominated by anything'. This verse deliberately plays with *exesti* and *exousia*: Thiselton attempts to convey this by translating ' "Liberty to do anything" – but I will not let anything take liberties with me' (Thiselton 2000, p. 461). The authority to do anything is related to being under the authority of Christ.

The Corinthians applied the principle of freedom to eating meat offered to idols. Paul agrees that this theological principal can be applied in this way but there is a greater principle still to be applied – that of love which, in the pattern of Christ crucified, **does not insist on its own way** (13:5).

In 10:24 he gives a formulation of the love command that is profoundly characteristic of his teaching. Paul consistently argues that the command to 'Love your neighbour' (Lev. 19:18) is a summary of the whole law (Rom. 13:9; Gal. 5:14). The Gospels record Jesus as approving a similar statement (Mark 12:31 and parallels). Paul often paraphrases or applies it in a formulation where love is interpreted as the behaviour that seeks to please another rather than self:

for example, **Love . . . does not insist on its own way** (1 Cor. 13:5).

Paul does not always cite the command as the love of 'a neighbour'. Sometimes he writes of loving 'one another'. For example, the **law of Christ** is to **bear one another's burdens** (Gal. 6:2). Compare this with Paul's statement about being **under Christ's law** which means becoming **all things to all people** (1 Cor. 9:21, 22); and with his exhortation that all members of the congregation should have **the same care for one another** (12:25).

In 1 Corinthians 10:24 (as in Rom. 13:8) he records the object of love (the person whose **advantage** should be sought) not as 'your neighbour' or even 'one another' but as **the other** (Greek, *ton heteron*). Whereas 'neighbour' suggests a person who is like ourselves, the **other** directs us to think about a person who is unlike ourselves: one, even, with whom we disagree (Barrett 1971, p. 240). Paul is supremely conscious that in the unity of *unlike* persons who are brought together in Christ, it is necessary for all to submit themselves voluntarily to the needs of the others, those who are not like them. This is the pattern of love and of the example of Christ. While this is a mutual, universal requirement, there may be a special demand on some: Paul's summary of similar issues in another letter is that, '*We who are strong* ought to put up with the failings of the weak and not to please ourselves' (Romans 15:1, my italics).

The illustration he goes on to give (1 Cor. 10:28ff.) shows Paul applying the theological principle in practical circumstances. The question to be asked in buying or eating food offered at pagan shrines is not, 'Is this forbidden or permitted?' because a believer has knowledge of the one God who makes all things, and, under Christ, all things are lawful. The question is rather, 'Is this building up or destroying sisters and brothers in the faith? Is this an act of love?' Paul has said that they may eat food in the house of an unbeliever, but this does not then become *a law*. They must therefore **Judge for [them]selves** as to whether they will choose to curb their own freedom. The scenario he suggests is not fully fleshed out: **someone** points out that the food has been **offered in sacrifice**. The implication is that this is a Christian whose consciousness of what is permitted in Christian life is not as clear and confident as Paul's or of some of the believers in Corinth. This means that the injunctions in 8:11–13 surely apply here.

It matters to Paul that this is not a subjection of his (or another Christian's) own consciousness of what is permitted or not. His freedom is voluntarily curbed by his perception of what might harm or build up another, and not because that other person is right. Paul maintains a fairly consistent emphasis on the voluntary nature of all such action (**Am I not free?**) because they are actions of love and not of command.

That the 'strong' should give way to the 'weak' is a reversal of normal hierarchies. In this particular situation, it is likely that the 'strong' were financially and socially more powerful than the 'weak' so Paul's exhortations reverse the usual social subordination of the poor to the rich. The cross has very practical, social implications: 'God chose what is foolish in the world to shame the wise; God chose what is weak in the world to shame the strong' (1 Cor. 1:27).

When you come together as a church

There is a second matter addressed in the letter, another question of a division in the congregation, which is likely to have been between believers of different social status.

📖 Reread I Corinthians 11:17–22.

What are the clues here that the divisions are related to matters of relative wealth or poverty?

Perhaps the basic division is revealed in 11:22: the people Paul is most directly addressing as **you** are those who have **homes to eat and drink in**, while some others are **those who have nothing**.

We do not know all there is to know about how Paul's congregations (or any others in the early decades of Christianity) worshipped and what they did when they celebrated the Lord's Supper. What is fairly clear is that believers can only have congregated after the daylight hours of work were over because there was no regular weekly holiday. This would be the time at which anyone who worked away from home would return for a meal.

Scholars are divided over whether at the Lord's Supper in a place like Corinth there would have been a full meal for the entire congregation as well as a sharing of bread and wine. At the last supper with

his disciples, Jesus seems to have shared bread with the new interpretative, sacramental words at the beginning of the meal when 'he
took his place at the table' (Luke 22:14) or 'while they were eating'
the meal (Mark 14:22), and then to have shared the cup of wine at
the end of the meal **after supper** (1 Cor. 11:25). Jesus and his disciples ate a meal in between the blessing of the bread and the sharing
of the cup. Did Christians carry on doing this, having a common meal
as well as bread and wine? Did the family and household of the house
where the congregation met have a private meal at the same time as
this common sharing of just bread and wine? Did everyone bring
food for their meal but were these separate meals which did not bring
them together in a common meal (of bread and wine) until the words
of institution? It is hard to be precise about the problem in Corinth
because we do not know exactly what usually took place. Theissen
argues that the Supper provided for all was solely bread and wine
(1982, p. 160) because of the injunction to 'eat at home'; Barrett
argues for a complete shared meal (1971, p. 277).

However, the knowledge that social historians can provide us of
other shared meals of the period may give us some insights into the
situation. Theissen suggests that there were at least two situations in
Roman society where it was accepted practice that at a common
meal, guests were treated differently (1982, pp. 147–62; cf. Meeks
1983, p. 68). One situation was in a *collegium*. *Collegia* were guilds of
tradespeople practising the same trade. When the members
assembled, office-holders might sometimes be allotted larger quan-
tities of food than ordinary members. Another situation was a
banquet held by a patron at which food of a different quality was
served to guests of different rank. (We haven't entirely left these
non-egalitarian practices behind: there are certainly colleges of
universities where those on the 'top table' are served a different
menu from those in the rest of the hall.) Theissen concludes that for
some Corinthians it would not have been at all strange to think that
common meals, involving people of varied social status, should
include food of varying quality. The variation of social status in a
Pauline congregation was more varied than in either of these two
instances, so perhaps some believers, or the host, assumed that these
differentiations of food would naturally occur in their common
meals.

There may also, or instead, have been a problem with workers coming later than the leisured, wealthier believers. Perhaps a common meal was provided but those who did not have to remain at work until sunset met and ate before the working believers arrived. This would accord with Paul's injunction to **wait** (11:33).

And the whole may have been compounded by the layout and size of the available accommodation (Murphy O'Connor 1983, pp. 153–61). A Roman villa's dining room or *triclinium* would not have held a congregation of more than forty: did the household's regular guests make their way to this well-provisioned inner sanctum while the rest (whose social standing had not made them accustomed to such a privilege) remained in the larger *atrium* outside?

The behaviour at the Lord's Supper, then, may be rooted in some status-specific expectations within a socially stratified culture. Whatever the precise situation of discord in the community, Paul finds it wholly unacceptable that the effect is that some **humiliate** others, and **show contempt for the church of God** (11:22). If the behaviour is in any way about status (apart from the 'status' of being a brother or sister for whom Christ died, 8:11) it conflicts with Paul's theology of the church where any such sharing must be an occasion of *unity* (10:17). It is also a matter of individual relationships where humiliation is not an expression of love or the self-giving of Christ crucified.

We need to keep in mind that the only reason there is a problem at all is because there is an expectation that this community of love encompasses people of different social strata on equal terms. In other *collegia* or at other feasts, there would be little point in complaining of unequal treatment – it would be accepted as normal and status-specific. Here, apparently, it should not.

Discerning the body

📖　Reread I Corinthians 11:22–34.

Is the problem regarding **discerning the body** (11:29) about
  (a) the bread as 'the Body of Christ' (11:24)
or
  (b) the community of believers as 'the Body of Christ' (cf. 10:17; 12:12–27)?
If it is the latter, what does **discerning the body** mean?

The solution to the discord awaits their own decision: 'Examine yourselves' (11:28). This accords with Christian freedom in love, and to Paul's teaching that the ultimate subjection is only to Christ (11:32). Clearly it is the members of the congregation who come from the upper strata who are most directly exhorted, yet the teaching is put in terms which the whole community can respond to: submission to one another is the role of all members. Similarly, the summary instructions are general: **Wait for one another. If you are hungry, eat at home** (11:33–4). In fact those **who have nothing** are not guilty of not waiting for other members: it is those who have the choice who must submit themselves in love to those who do not. Nevertheless, Paul reminds the whole community of their calling to give way to 'one another'.

Whether or not the discernment **of the body** (11:29) is *also* relevant to the later church debates about the substance of the consecrated bread, Paul certainly meant that discerning the congregation of believers as the Body of Christ, and treating them accordingly, is a matter for them to **judge** for themselves (11:31) lest they be judged by God. It is a striking example of the wholly practical application of Paul's theology: the outworking of the proclamation of the crucified Messiah includes the basic courtesy of waiting for people. Once again Paul includes himself in the exhortation rather than standing beyond his correspondents: **if we judged ourselves** . . . (11:31).

Reflecting on the message and the method

In both the Corinthian cases, Paul deplores the (oppressive) exercise of social or financial advantage. He addresses his admonitions effectively to the 'strong': he and they are to subordinate themselves for the building up of the whole community. This is a reversal of the social stratifications, though the governing idea is of mutual subordination, of each to all. Gerhardsson claims that Paul 'whose individual ethics were so radical, showed . . . little radicalism in his social ethics' (1982, p. 88). We have studied two passages that challenge this view.

No one is in a social vacuum, however, and Paul must have been defined to some extent, as we all are, by our social background and experience. It is an interesting piece of detective work to try to trace the identity of the people with whom Paul seems to have felt particular affinity or to have shared a social context. In 1 Corinthians

1:14–16, he mentions the names of three men whose households, he says, are the only ones he himself baptised: Crispus, Gaius and Stephanas.

Crispus, we learn from Acts 18:8, is **the official of the synagogue** in Corinth, a position which means he was a man of some financial substance.

Gaius, we learn from Romans 16:23, is **host** to Paul **and to the whole church** (in Corinth). That suggests at least the means to provide for guests and a large house to meet in.

Stephanas, we learn from 1 Corinthians itself, has **devoted himself to the service of the saints** (16:15). Paul wants the Corinthians in turn to **give recognition to such persons** (16:18) and to put themselves **at the service of such people** (16:16). This is a mutual service, but not entirely symmetrical: what was their service to Stephanas, and what was his to them? He has the means and independence to travel, and is possibly another patron of the Corinthian congregations.

It is then inescapable that the three particular connections Paul owns in Corinth were among the 'strong' and privileged of those congregations. This is not reprehensible – it was very likely to be the case – but it can make us aware that, from Paul, we are getting a view from a particular position when it comes to poverty and wealth. We will want to ask similar questions when we look at issues concerning gender and slavery.

Suggestions for further reading

Clarke, Andrew, 1993. *Secular and Christian Leadership in Corinth*, Leiden, Brill

Malherbe, A.J., 1983. *Social Aspects of Early Christianity*, Philadelphia, Fortress

Meeks, Wayne A., 1983. *The First Urban Christians*, Yale, YUP

Theissen, Gerd, 1982. *The Social Setting of Pauline Christianity*, Edinburgh, T&T Clark

Wilson, Robert McL., 1993. 'Gnosticism', in B. M. Metzger *et al.* (eds.), *The Oxford Companion to the Bible*, Oxford, OUP, pp. 255–6

Witherington, Ben, 1995. *Conflict and Community in Corinth: socio-rhetorical commentary on 1 and 2 Corinthians*, Carlisle, Paternoster Press

In this chapter, reference was also made to the following works

Barrett, C.K., 1971. *The First Epistle to The Corinthians*, London, Black

Fiorenza, E. Schüssler, 1983. *In Memory of Her: a feminist theological reconstruction of Christian origins*, London, SCM

Gerhardsson, Birger, 1982. *The Ethos of the Bible*, London, SCM

O'Connor, J. Murphy, 1983. *St Paul's Corinth*, Wilmington, Glazier

Thiselton, A.C., 2000. *First Epistle to the Corinthians*, Carlisle, Paternoster Press

Wire, A.C., 1990. *The Corinthian Women Prophets*, Minneapolis, Fortress

CHAPTER 7

'Conjugal rights': the freedoms and authority of marriage partners

1 Corinthians 7

The aim of this chapter is to see how Paul's Christology and eschato-logy impact on his teaching about relationships in marriage. The questions are related to those examined in Chapter 6 about whether Paul's teaching supports or subverts a social system which gave higher status to those of greater wealth. Do marriage partners mutu-ally give way to one another in the pattern of the cross, or is a social status of wives, as subordinate to their husbands, reflected in Paul's expectations?

Men, women and marriage

It was probably the first question asked about each of us on our emer-gence from the womb: 'Is it a boy or a girl?' Even in families or societies where there is no radical discrimination against one or the other (and there are many), this is still a question asked as if all other matters were secondary to the binary division of gender.

Within that strong awareness of two sexes, a wide range of atti-tudes distinguishing between them is observable. A society where women were *radically* less privileged than men is a short number of decades from contemporary Britain: within the lifetime of some women and men alive today the electorate was entirely male, and women who campaigned for the right to vote were assaulted and imprisoned. There are still great disparities between women and men in salaries, property, management, political office and other factors in the 'developed' world. Opinion is divided (and not just on gender lines) as to whether some or all of these differences are discrimina-tory and oppressive or reflections of choice and difference.

The normative social and legal institution in this society is still (though challenged) formed by marriage. Here is one of the arenas

where a binary difference of gender is to most participants essential
to the union, but husbands and wives may still have a wide range of
expectations about the role of their spouse. We are now seeing,
perhaps, more variations in models of marriage, where roles undertaken by wife or husband counter the tradition in which the public
sphere belongs to men and the domestic sphere to women.

Today's churches are divided about the place of women in
ordained ministries, but that will be matter for Chapter 9.

A conflict movement

In the Roman Empire, the basic pattern of hierarchical, patriarchal
authority and power was established and near-universal. Wayne
Meeks comments: 'The hierarchical pattern of the family, in which
the male was always superior to the female, as surely as parents to
children and masters to slaves, was deeply entrenched in law and
custom and its erosion constantly deplored by rhetorical moralists
and the satirists' (1983, p. 23).

However, alongside dominant theories justifying the status quo,
there were some contemporary philosophical justifications for
considering women the equals of men. In practice too, there were
exceptions to subordinate-womankind. There were remarkable ones
like the powerful Empress Livia. More mundanely, there were
women active in commerce and manufacture, women involved in
independent litigation, women receiving municipal honours as
benefactors and city officials, women acting as founders and patrons
of men's clubs, and women travelling with their own slaves and
helpers.

We saw in the previous chapter that sociology offers the term
'status-inconsistency' to describe individuals or groups who might
have a low social status in one respect but exhibit some power or
authority in other respects. In Paul's congregations a number of
women exhibited some sort of status-inconsistency. Some exercised
charismatic functions like prayer and prophecy (1 Cor. 11:2–16).
Others Paul claims as undertaking various roles in the church as his
fellow workers, evangelists, teachers, patrons, helpers. There is quite
a list in Romans 16: Phoebe, a **deacon** and **benefactor**; Prisca,
who work[s] with me; Mary, **who has worked very hard
among you**; Junia, **prominent among the apostles**; Tryphaena,

Tryphosa and Persis, **workers in the Lord** (Rom. 16:1, 3, 6, 7, 12).

There does seem to have been a reluctance in the history of the Church to acknowledge that these women had roles of much significance or status in the earliest churches. You may find even recent translations that call Phoebe 'deaconess' and 'helper' rather than **deacon** and **benefactor**/patron. Junia, whom Paul calls an **apostle** (see Glossary item in Chapter 5), was for centuries held to be a man called Junias, though the name as a woman's name is much better attested.

We noted in the previous chapter that within the larger society of the Greco-Roman world, the Christian movement was a 'conflict' movement because it was in tension with some of the hierarchical institutions of that society and did not withdraw from the rest of society. One of the status-inconsistencies we might notice in the situation of women believers in Corinth is between their status as married women in pagan households and their status in the Christian community.

Each man, each woman

📖   Reread I Corinthians 7:1–7.

How many of the injunctions in these verses are addressed to men and how many to women?

The first issue Paul addresses about married relationships is sex. Who first said or wrote, **It is well for a man not to touch a woman** (7:1)? It seems to have been a phrase in the Corinthians' letter. Is this an example of the Corinthians' asceticism – even a denial of the goodness of the created order of matter and the body such as that in the later Gnostic movements (see Glossary item 'Gnosticism' in Chapter 6)? Or could this be one of the times when the Corinthians have quoted back at Paul something he has said or written to them? If so, perhaps it was in his letter about not associating with the sexually immoral (5:9). Either way the effect of the teaching seems to be that one of the partners in married couples was refusing to have sex with their husband or wife (those who **deprive one another**, 7:5).

In 7:7, Paul seems to be saying that he himself has the **gift** of celibacy (whether he is now unmarried, married, widowed or 'separated'), and however positively he writes about marriage, he seems to have a personal preference for the non-married state. Even in his positive statements about sex here, he seems to see sex within marriage as a remedy for those without the **self-control** (7:5) to abstain and who might otherwise indulge in **sexual immorality** (7:2). Abstention for a time (both husband and wife agreeing to do so) he sees as valuable in promoting prayer (7:5), which seems to imply that having sex might somehow impede a spiritual life. It is thus not impossible to imagine Paul having said or written such a thing as he quotes in 7:1, though not with any gnosticising dualism behind the idea. If so, it may well have provoked the Corinthians to seek clarification: is abstention from sex desirable in the order of salvation?

Whether he or the Corinthians originated the phrase, Paul's response is revealing in its rigorous equality about wives and husbands, even if it is half-hearted about the value of the physical relationship. In contrast to the male-centred quotation which offers no corresponding statement that 'It is well for a woman not to touch a man', Paul carefully repeats every injunction in 7:2–5, in order to make sure that husband and wife acknowledge equal obligations. It involves some striking statements. That **the wife does not have authority over her own body, but the husband does,** would have raised no eyebrows in the Roman world: that was precisely the status of a woman in marriage. The reciprocal statement that **likewise the husband does not have authority over his own body, but the wife does**, is an incomparably more radical idea in Paul's world. It suggests two things: an equality, at some level, between women and men in Paul's view, and bodily expression of the relationship, sex, as one area of life where this equality counted.

Some commentators argue that the mutuality of married partners is only for the sexual side of conjugal relationships. By encouraging equality here Paul is not necessarily claiming that women have the same **authority** (freedom and accountability) in other areas of marriage that their husbands have. This passage alone might not give us a model of wholly egalitarian marriage.

If she consents to live with him

📖 Reread I Corinthians 7:8–16.

Who is portrayed as exercising choices in these verses?

To what degree is the Lord's command, or Paul's exhortation, authoritative for those choices?

Here we have one of the instances where Paul cites what we know from the Gospels (Mark 10:9 and parallels) to be something handed on as part of Jesus' teaching. In Chapter 3, we saw that such instances may be very rare; we should relate it too to the discussion of Paul's own authority in Chapter 5.

Paul distinguishes between Jesus' teaching (of husbands and wives not separating) and what he, Paul, adds to it (of the circumstance of a Christian being married to an **unbeliever**).

One thing this tells us is that some married women in Corinth had become converts to Christianity without the consent of their (pagan) husbands. It seems very likely that male or female believers married to pagans might well have questioned whether being united to Christ (cf. 6:17) they should cease to be united with their spouses. Paul makes no arguments about any subjection of wives to husbands or women to men in terms of the social order. First they are subject to the **command** of Christ (7:10). Second they are subject to the needs of the other person, a voluntary subordination which once again bears no relation to social stratifications. The Christian partner in a mixed marriage is to give their pagan spouse the decision about the continuance of the marriage.

In practice this must have been more difficult for Christian women than for Christian men. More on this shortly when we look at Paul's advice to widows not to remarry (7:39–40).

It is the more remarkable that Paul urges this submission to their spouses since on the whole he prefers and advocates the marriage-free Christian life. It is, however, wholly consistent with his belief that all Christian submission reflects submission to Christ's Lordship that, in **the end**, God may be **all in all** (15:28). This is expressed here by God's call to peace (7:15) and by the motivation that the unbelieving partner too might come to acknowledge the Lordship of Christ (7:16).

As in 7:2–5 there are carefully reciprocal statements about women matching those about men. As with 7:4, the result is an overturning of part of religious and social tradition. In the reciprocal teaching that the unbelieving husband is consecrated through his wife and the unbelieving wife is consecrated through her husband (7:14) Paul may be assigning to Christian wives a power traditionally bestowed only on husbands: 'in Judaism it is invariably the woman who is consecrated [i.e. taken in marriage] as spouse by the man' (Daube in Fiorenza 1983, p. 222).

The condition in which you were called

📖 Reread I Corinthians 7:17–24.

Paul interrupts his teaching about married couples. What other groups of people does he introduce into the chapter?

📖 Read Galatians 3:27–8.

Identify the verses of I Corinthians 7 which deal with each of the three pairs of people in Galatians 3:28.

📖 Reread I Corinthians 7:17–24.

What are the indications that the same 'formula' is in Paul's mind here that he uses in Galatians 3? And what is missing?

Why does Paul shift his attention from husbands and wives to circumcised and uncircumcised men (male Jews and Gentiles) and then to slaves and freed or free people? He will return to questions of marriage in 7:25–39.

It is possible that Paul is aware of slaves among the Corinthian believers who, because of his teaching of the new order and their freedom in Christ are expecting a change of their social and legal status outside the church (Bassler in Meeks 1983, p. 219). There were also questions in the early decades of Christianity about Gentile men being circumcised in order to conform to Jewish law. However, it seems much more likely that these two pairs of people are introduced into his teaching about marriage as comparable examples of believers who, like the married or unmarried, should **remain in the condition in which** they **were called.**

📂 GLOSSARY : *'Male and female' (Galatians 3:28)*

In Galatians 3:27–8, Paul cites what may have been the core of a Pauline or pre-Pauline baptismal confession:

> As many of you as were baptized into Christ have clothed yourselves with Christ. There is no longer Jew or Greek, there is no longer slave or free, there is no longer male and female; for all of you are one in Christ Jesus.

His use of this in 1 Corinthians 12:13 again with reference to unity and baptism makes it very likely indeed that in 1 Corinthians 7 too he has this baptismal formula in mind. The absence of **male and female** in the second reference in 1 Corinthians 12 may be because he has dealt with complex issues of male and female relations in 1 Corinthians 7, and because there were vexed issues in the community concerning the behaviour of women and men in worship (1 Cor. 11 and 14 – see Chapter 9).

In 1 Corinthians 7 though, the **male and female** pairing is the subject of the teaching to which the other pairings are (on this occasion) subsidiary examples.

Clearly, for Paul, husbands should remain husbands and wives remain wives (on the whole) so the relationship of this teaching to the assertion in Galatians 3:28 that **there is no longer male and female . . . in Christ** needs to be examined.

The text of Galatians does not read, **Jew or Greek . . . slave or free . . . *man or woman*** as we might predict following the pattern of the first two pairs. The third pair is linked with and (*kai*) instead of or (*oude*) – though this distinction is not acknowledged in all translations. Further the words **male** and **female** are used instead of 'man' and 'woman'.

Another verse of the Bible has the same phrase:

> So God created humankind in his image, in the image of God he created them; *male and female* he created them. (Gen. 1:27)

The baptismal formula uses this quotation from Genesis because, surely, here too the relationship with God is primary, and the relationship between the sexes is secondary.

In Genesis 1:27 the phrase **male and female** introduces the theme of procreation and fertility, in the order of creation. In Galatians too the pairing is about husbands and wives, that is, men and women in their married role and status, but in the new order of salvation. Elisabeth Schüssler Fiorenza argues as follows:

> As such Galatians 3:28c does not assert that there are no longer men and women in Christ, but that patriarchal marriage – and sexual relationships between

male and female – is no longer constitutive of the new community in Christ. Irrespective of their procreative capacities and of the social roles connected with them, persons will be full members of the Christian movement in and through baptism. (1983, p. 211)

We saw an instance of this in 1 Corinthians 7:12–16 where it is clear that some married women in Corinth had become believers without the consent of their husbands. **There is no longer male and female** in Christ. That is, a woman's status in Christ is not dependent on her role as a wife.

Just as the unequal social status accorded to rich and poor was not to be reflected in their status and worth in the Christian community (as in the matter of the Lord's Supper in 1 Corinthians 11) so **slaves** and the **free** were not to be deemed different in Christ. Paul's letters to the Galatians and the Romans testify to his insistence that **Jews** and **Gentiles** were equally recipients of salvation by grace and through faith. These parallels used in 1 Corinthians 7 reinforce the teaching in the rest of that chapter that a woman's participation in Christ was not dependent on her husband or on her single status; and a man's similarly was not dependent on his wife or his unmarried state.

Remain in the condition in which you were called may be a teaching more readily assented to by a free person than a slave, or by someone happily married or happily single than by someone with, say, a domineering spouse. We will return to slaves in the Corinthian church in Chapter 10. We will see in the next passage that Paul's view on anyone's present **condition** is explicitly related to his eschatological belief that **the present form of this world is passing away** (7:31).

In view of the impending crisis

Reread 1 Corinthians 7:25–8.

Whom does Paul address in these verses? What can you infer about the implied 'you'?

Reread 1 Corinthians 7:29–31.

Paul's eschatology has sometimes been characterised as 'already' but 'not yet' (see Glossary item 'Eschatology' in Chapter 4). Would you relate Paul's exhortations here to a 'realised' or 'imminent' eschatology?

📖 Reread I Corinthians 7:32–40.

How many of these verses have men as the subject, and how many have women as the subject?

The second **Now concerning** . . . (7:25) may introduce a related but distinct issue raised by the Corinthians in the light of Paul's teaching to them. The **virgins** in this passage are probably previously unmarried people who are engaged to be married, and who in that 'halfway' state might reasonably ask, which **condition** should I **remain in**, single or married? Paul advises them to remain unmarried (7:26) but to remain celibately in the betrothed relationship (7:37). He permits marriage in these circumstances, which he sees as a concession again to a sex drive (7:36) – not sinful, but, Paul seems to suggest, a remedy for those whose **desire** is not **under control**. He really is not wholehearted about sex and marriage (7:38).

The *occasion* of the question from the Corinthians may be indicated in 7:36. Here the NRSV translates the same word for **virgin** (*parthenos*) as **fiancée** because the Greek reads 'his virgin' so it is surely here a young woman engaged to a particular man. The possessive 'his' or 'her' can shift or establish the range of a word in this way. The same happens with other Greek words: *andros* means 'man' but also 'husband'; *gunē* means 'woman' but also 'wife'. A sentence which says 'his woman' or 'her man' confirms that it is about a wife and a husband. Otherwise, there can be an ambiguity. (More of this in Chapter 9.) It may be because the question comes from or about a particular man in this situation that this section, 7:36–8, abandons the balanced address to women as well as to men: here the **anyone** and the **someone** is male.

There is some debate about the eschatological urgency of Paul's teaching in this passage and it is not unrelated to different Christian views about the authority or inerrancy of Scripture. If Paul thought that it was **well** for unmarried or betrothed people to **remain** unmarried (7:26) because **the appointed time has grown short** (7:29) before the end comes (15:24), then, two thousand years later, we might look back on this as bad advice. *If* Paul expected an end so imminent that marriage for the begetting of children would be purposeless, then he was wrong about that. We will think more about the authority for Christians of Paul's letters in Chapter 11.

Paul's language here does seem characteristic of the apocalyptic eschatology, and *imminent* expectation of a catastrophic end, of parts of the New Testament. Paul's anxiety that those who marry will experience distress may reflect the same idea that we find in Mark 13:17–19: 'Woe to those who are pregnant and to those who are nursing infants in those days! Pray that it may not be in winter. For in those days there will be suffering.' Some commentators argue that this is not Paul's meaning here. For these (see, for example, the argument in Thiselton 2000, pp. 571–6) the **impending crisis** (7:26) is rather the *present* crisis (the Greek, *enestōsan,* could mean either) which encompasses the present reality of the believer's life in Christ, including their share in his sufferings. The meaning, in this interpretation, of **the appointed time has grown short** is not that the end is coming soon but that the appointed time is *shorter*; that is, the end-times *have begun*.

The anxieties which Paul goes on to consider in 7:32–5 do not seem to be eschatological woes. Rather he sees the concerns of **pleasing** a husband or wife to be a hindrance in **devotion to the Lord**. This is the only time when the voluntary submission of one believer to another person is seen as an obstacle in their voluntary submission to Christ. It is an argument that has been used in regulating for the celibacy of parish priests. It is slightly puzzling that Paul argues in quite this way when a married couple like Aquila and Prisca (16:19) stood high in his estimation of fellow workers.

Just as Paul advises a separated woman not to remarry (7:11), so he advises a widow to remain non-married, though **she is free to marry anyone she wishes** (7:39). It is another instance of the authority which Paul credits each believer as having: the decision and freedom is theirs and not Paul's or anyone else's. However, his advice is in radical opposition to the social hierarchy of the Roman world. It is counter to the social hierarchy that Paul advises believers, and particularly that he advises women (7:39–40), to remain free from marriage. Calling this 'a frontal assault on the intentions of existing law and the general cultural ethos', Fiorenza continues: 'his advice to women to remain non-married was a severe infringement of the right

of the *paterfamilias* since, according to Roman law, a woman remained
under the tutorship of her father and family, even after she married'
(1983, pp. 225–6).

The implications are quite far-reaching. Since girls were usually
married in their teens and could be married from the age of twelve,
and since it was not at all unusual for their husbands to be much
older, then Paul is giving this advice, potentially, to very young
widows and not only to older women. Fiorenza points out that this
offered a possibility for 'ordinary' women to become independent in
a way that conflicted with the expectation of the society outside the
church.

It also made them vulnerable in a society where most women were
financially dependent on a man, and we will see how the post-Pauline
tradition responded to this early radicalism in Chapter 10.

Reflecting on the message and the method

Paul's explicit expression of the nature but also the limits of his own
authority in 7:25 offers a confirmation of his boldness to command
and his preference for appealing on the basis of love (cf. Philem.
8–9): 'I have no command of the Lord, but I give my opinion as one
who by the Lord's mercy is trustworthy.' His belief in the Lordship
of Christ does not lead to a moral code made up of Jesus' commands.
He cites Jesus' teaching, and is explicit about whether a teaching is
his own or from Jesus, but he is not limited to it. Similarly, the
Corinthians are not limited to a teaching of Paul's but, having heard
it, make their own judgements. The final verses of the chapter are
revealing: 'she is free to marry anyone she wishes, only in the Lord.
But in my judgement she is more blessed if she remains as she is'
(7:39–40).

Paul adds a rider: 'And I think that I too have the Spirit of God'
(7:40). He endorses their possession of the Spirit of God which gives
them (women and men) an authority like his to make judgements
about doctrine and practice. He reminds them, however, that they are
not alone in this. From the opening of the letter he has congratu-
lated them on their spiritual gifts (1:7) and also called their attention
to their unity with the rest of the churches (1:2).

It reminds us that his correspondents are free to disagree with
Paul, and in doing so claim the same source of authority as he, and

Paul acknowledges this. Indeed it was he who first taught them this and brought them this freedom. He seems particularly conscious here that their judgements may well not quite reflect his own. He knows that the Body is diverse: 'But each has a particular gift from God, one having one kind and another a different kind' (7:7). We will now look at 1 Corinthians 12 where this is a core matter.

Suggestions for further reading

Clark, Gillian, 1993. *Women in Late Antiquity: pagan and Christian lifestyles*, Clarendon

Evans, R.C., 1994. 'Women in the New Testament', in Isherwood and McEwan (eds.), *A Dictionary of Christian Feminist Theology*, Sheffield, SAP

Fiorenza, E. Schüssler, 1983. *In Memory of Her: a feminist theological reconstruction of Christian origins*, London, SCM, pp. 160–334

Witherington, Ben, 1991. *Women in the Earliest Churches*, Cambridge, CUP

In this chapter, reference was also made to the following works

Thiselton, A.C., 2000, *The First Epistle to the Corinthians*, Carlisle, Paternoster Press

Meeks, W., 1983. *The First Urban Christians*, Yale, YUP

CHAPTER 8

'When you come together': authority and equality in worship

1 Corinthians 12–14

In this chapter we will question how Paul's Christology and eschatology impact on his teaching about worship and in particular what sort of authority or leadership was exercised or acknowledged in the community. This will be related to the questions in Chapter 5 about Paul's own authority and the Corinthians' freedom to make judgements.

Patterns of ministry

Some of the large Christian denominations today have ministers who are ordained into the 'orders' of deacon, priest or bishop. Others have members called elders and deacons. Other denominations or congregations begin with forms of leadership which arise partly from acknowledged charismatic gifts. These are all titles or functions that derive from words and practices in the New Testament. The fact that different denominations today have different ideas about orders of leadership and ministry is a clue to us that the first churches developed a number of different practices, and that the New Testament passages that refer to them are interpreted in different ways.

In the opening to the Letter to the Philippians, Paul mentions two groups of people called 'overseers' or 'guardians' (the Greek word is *episkopos* which has given us the English word 'bishop') and 'helpers' or 'ministers' (the Greek work is *diakonos* and gives us the word 'deacon'). In a later letter in the post-Pauline tradition, these two sets of people are clearly church officers with a hierarchical status in the community and regulations are given for how they should fulfil their roles (1 Tim. 3). Some readers assume that what is written in 1 Timothy must have been the case from the beginning of Paul's churches, and that when Paul used the terms in Philippians 1:1 he meant exactly what the *later* letter describes. Others see this hierarchical pattern of office-holders as a later development, after Paul, deriving but differing from an earlier more egalitarian model of community where some women and some men may have had a particular function but not a different status.

It is likely that different churches and collections of churches had different practices. The community of John's Gospel may have had little interest in institutional authority and no hierarchy of office-holders. The author of Acts, on the other hand, may reflect the practice of the Jerusalem churches, which perhaps modelled themselves a little on Jewish synagogues. He refers (Acts 14:23; 20:17) to Paul appointing 'elders' (the Greek word is *presbuteros*, giving us 'presbyter'). This word seems to carry a sense of status with it – and not merely the naming of a function. It is not a term Paul seems to use himself, and it may not have been his practice to appoint officers in quite this way – the author of Acts is perhaps describing a custom and structure with which, later than Paul, he was himself familiar.

There is no doubt that Paul valued 'order' in Christian community. At the same time he founded and pastored communities where charismatic gifts were not just exercised by one or more 'leaders' but by most or all of the members of the church. Who then were the leaders or ministers in Paul's first churches, and what did they do?

📖 Reread I Corinthians 12 and 14.

What do these chapters tell us about the kind of worship that Paul's churches experienced? What happened and who took part?

Note that in a summary of his argument about the conduct of worship at the end, I Corinthians 14:39–40, Paul brings together both a concern for order and an encouragement of charismatic enthusiasm.

Now concerning spiritual gifts

The **Now concerning** . . . (12:1) alerts us to the specific occasion of this part of the letter in enquiries which the Corinthians have directed to Paul (7:1). If they have written to him asking about spiritual gifts, what was it that they had asked or told him? It may be useful to recall the summary message right at the opening of the letter, **I appeal to you . . . that all of you should be in agreement and that there should be no divisions among you** (1:10), because there is a very clear focus on unity in 1 Corinthians 12. What is the subject of the particular disunity Paul deals with here?

Unless Paul is jumping from one partly related issue to another, then we need to look for ideas that hold together the matter of 12:2–3, 12:4–11 and 12:14–26, etc., and of 1 Corinthians 13 and 14, and also for teaching that bears some relation to the whole letter and its concerns (in an application of the hermeneutical circle).

If 12:3 was to mean anything to the first audience of this letter, it is possible that someone at Corinth must have said at least one of the two things Paul quotes, **Let Jesus be cursed** or **Jesus is Lord**, and that the speaker's relation to the Holy Spirit was then questioned by members of the community. In the plausible scenario created by Hans Frör (1995, pp. 62–72) it was the first of these: someone, formerly used to ecstatic utterance in the worship of other deities (**idols**, 12:2), said during an ecstatic utterance, **Let Jesus be cursed**. However, we might connect this verse more closely with what follows if we assume it is the second quotation that is the key statement: that Paul is insisting that *all* who say **Jesus is Lord** should be seen as being activated by the Holy Spirit.

The passage that follows, 12:4–11, lists a number of different **gifts, services, activities** (all those three words are used). These are all things that may have occurred in public worship (though it is not clear exactly what acts of **faith** Paul refers to in 12:9). Was this made a point of contention among the Corinthians? Did they think that some of these activities were inspired by the Spirit and others were not, or were of much less value? Or was it more a question of personalities than of activities? Were there certain people of standing in the congregation who impressively and regularly demonstrated ecstatic charismatic gifts? Perhaps when some other members of the congregation demonstrated the same or different charismatic activities, these were thought to be usurping the function of accepted leaders whose perceived role it was to speak or act in the Spirit in public worship.

📁 GLOSSARY : *Gifts of Tongues and Prophecy*

The phenomenon of 'speaking in tongues' or glossolalia is known variously in a number of religious traditions and its appearance in the New Testament can be seen in cultural, sociological context (Stendahl 1977) and as a human psychological phenomenon (Theissen 1987, pp. 74–114, 292–341) without disparagement to belief in its operation as part of a relationship with the divine.

The Christian understanding of it as a gift of the Spirit is written about explicitly in the New Testament only in I Corinthians 12–14 and in Acts. It has been experienced at different times through the history of the Church, sometimes as part of forms of revival, as with the contemporary charismatic movement.

Acts 2 represents it as prophecy, as being understood by hearers, each in their own language: this seems to have been peculiar to the representation of the Pentecost event. Elsewhere in Acts, as with Paul in I Corinthians, it is assumed that people will not understand someone speaking in tongues, unless they have the gift of interpretation. Similarly, in I Corinthians, the speakers in tongues are themselves not usually able to understand their own utterance.

It is likely that Paul's (and Paul's congregations') understanding of 'prophecy' was not merely instant, brief prophetic utterances, but could also be, effectively, pastoral preaching. The inspired words need not have been merely spontaneous but considered, situated, even prepared: 'applied theological teaching . . . to build the church' (Thiselton 2000, p. 826; cf. Gillespie 1994, pp. 97–164).

Glossolalia shares in the nature of prophecy, as a revelation of a message or insight from God, but which requires the further gift of interpretation, in the speaker or another hearer, in order to become actual prophecy. Paul exhorts those who speak in tongues to pray also for the power to interpret (I Cor. 14:13–19).

Less respectable members

The suggestion that there was a question of perceived personal or institutional status at stake connects with the theme of the next passage, where Paul uses the now famous image of the **Body** of Christ (12:12–27). It is a fundamental in Paul's theology which is possibly reflected even in the traditions of his call, recorded in Acts. The voice of Jesus (and this must reflect Paul's own account of the experience) says to him, not 'Why are you persecuting my followers?' but 'Why are you persecuting *me*?' (Acts 9:4; 22:7; 26:14, my italics). It is a fascinating insight into Paul's belief in the identification of Christ with those, in Paul's phrase, who are **in Christ**.

He was not the first to use the idea of a society as a body made up of interdependent members. There was already a history of such a metaphor, used against division and factionalism in society or state. However, Paul's argument is very different from the usual use.

📖　Reread I Corinthians 12:20–5.

If the analogy is that members of the congregation are like members of a human body, what is the recommended relation of **less respectable** and **more respectable** members?

In other classical speeches and writings (for examples, see Witherington 1995, pp. 253–4) the image is employed as an exhortation directed to those of lower social status. The idea is that the state will be unified and harmonious if the lower orders submit to the authority of the ruling classes. This is the *opposite* of what Paul says. He makes the striking observation that although, or because, people (in his society as in many others) regard their genitals or other parts of their bodies as not respectable, they take great care to treat them with respect. Even if other parts of our bodies are uncovered, our **inferior** parts are not often treated with such carelessness. Our hands, for example, may be more **respectable** but we do not need to give them special treatment (12:24). (Indeed, given a choice between wearing only gloves or only underwear, most of us would go for underwear every time!) This striking paradox means that it is not the factious behaviour of people of low social standing or of less importance in the church that Paul is writing against – it is the attitude of those to whom respect is usually given which needs to change. It is they who are being factious in their treatment of people whom they regard as of less worth or use. Remember that there was considerable economic and social disparity between different members of the church, and that Roman Corinth probably had a very status-conscious ethos.

This is absolutely in line with Paul's earlier exhortations that the 'strong' should consider the needs of the 'weak' and not disturb their consciences in the matter of meat offered to idols (8:7–13), and that at the Lord's Supper the rich who have homes should wait for those who have nothing (11:17–33). Here again is Paul's overarching message of **Christ crucified**, where imitation of Christ means submitting to the needs of others in the pattern of the cross. Not only is this not the submission of the low to the high – rather the submission of all for the common good – but the instances are regularly of the submission of the higher to the lower (measured by economic and social status, or ecclesiastical importance, or both).

God has appointed

In summary then, the people who have some sort of importance or standing are exhorted to honour other members of the church, especially those whose standing is lower. The context seems to mean that they should implement this in terms of the valuing of spiritual gifts demonstrated in public worship.

Paul then gives a second list of gifts 12:28–30. There are several parallels in this with the previous list in 12:8–10, but this second list seems to push at the boundaries of what gifts are exercised for the church purely in public worship, and brings in Paul's own most distinctive role with them as apostle. Neither list is meant to be exhaustive, and it seems that there was not one single accepted list ranked in order of importance. However, this second list is headed by three roles labelled, **first**, **second** and **third**. Some commentators claim that this is a ranking of authority: apostles are to be considered as more important than prophets and prophets more important than teachers. Others believe that the order refers to the sequence of events in founding a church, from the proclamation of the gospel through to the instruction and edification of the members, rather than to the status given to the individuals who carry out these different functions.

Paul has written about these different functions before.

📖 Reread 1 Corinthians 3:5–9.

Is Paul's teaching here that he as the community's apostle is **first**, and Apollos as a later teacher of the community is of less

account? What are the parallels between this passage and I
Corinthians 12?

After the first three roles in 12:28, the list is not of the person or the
role (e.g. a 'prophet') but of the gift or function (e.g. **prophecy**),
again indicating that these lists are illustrative of *varieties* of gifts, not
hierarchies of the people who have them. Believers might find themselves in more than one place on the list: Paul was apostle to the
Corinthians but he also demonstrated other gifts in the lists (e.g.
14:18).

Two things are new to the second list: **forms of assistance** and
forms of leadership. It is an interesting pairing, assistance and
leadership, in terms of our questions about authority and equality in
the community. **Leadership**, if that is what is implied by the second
of the two, is probably specific to particular functions rather than
meaning generically 'a leader of the congregation'. The word (Greek,
kubernēseis) is thought by some to mean (here) 'administration' and by
others 'guidance' as in spiritual counselling. The NRSV has chosen a
fairly literal word that might mean either. The NRSV also rightly gives
plural phrases, **forms of**, rather than merely 'assistance' or 'leadership' as if there was a single structure of service and leadership.

Love is patient

Before tackling his main example of gifts of the Spirit in worship, to
be used or constrained for the common good, Paul first inserts
within this discussion the poetic, even hymnic, passage concerning
love.

📖   Reread I Corinthians 13.

What resonances are there between this passage and the discussion in I Corinthians 12 (and 14) about how the Corinthians
should view themselves and their gifts of the Spirit?

It is wholly apt that in a letter headed, **I appeal to you . . . that all
of you be in agreement and that there be no divisions**, Paul
should speak at length of love. It is another indication that this letter
is a literary and theological unity, and not a compilation of miscellan-

eous teachings. In the closing of the letter, Paul summarises his whole teaching with, **Let all that you do be done in love** (16:14), and uses **love** (Greek: *agapē*) again in his closing greeting (16:24).

There are two particular qualities of love to pick out in our current discussion, and they are central to Paul's christological and eschatological message. One is that love **does not insist on its own way** (13:4). It is fundamental for Paul that the way of the cross (**We proclaim Christ crucified**, 1:23) is one where the other person's needs, or the needs of the community, take precedence. This is central to the discussion of 1 Corinthians 12 and 14, but also to the whole outlook expounded from 1 Corinthians 8 onwards.

The second quality is that because all things are **passing away**, neither **knowledge** nor **prophecy**, nor anything else that might confer status, is more than **partial** or will endure beyond the end. **Love** only, with **faith** and **hope**, is eternal. The paradox of the cross is that it is the weakness of giving way that is triumphant and enduring. Love is the pattern of the cross; love is the pattern of the end.

The greater gifts

Paul has suggested a hierarchy of gifts in 12:31: **Strive for the greater gifts**. However, immediately in chapter 14, we see what he might mean by this. **One who prophesies is greater than one who speaks in tongues, unless someone interprets** (14:5). It is therefore not that a gift is necessarily greater in itself, but can be greater or less in the way it is or is not used for the great purpose – **for the common good** (12:7), **so that the church may be built up** (14:5). Rather than establishing a hierarchy of gifts and offices, the whole thrust of this passage is anti-hierarchical – a subordination of each to the good of all.

The focus of 1 Corinthians 14 on speaking in tongues and interpreting tongues suggests that this must have been at the heart of the situation Paul began to address in more general terms in 1 Corinthians 12. I raised the question, above, that there may have been people of rank or importance in the community who exercised charismatic gifts who did not value the charismatic contributions of other members of the community deemed less important. If that is so, then it seems that the gifts that were valued by these individuals –

and possibly by all the community – were gifts of tongues. Both of the lists of gifts had included **tongues,** and **interpretation of tongues** is in the first list and in the questions that follow the second list. Paul's question in 12:30, **Do all speak in tongues?** is in a form that requires the answer 'No' – it was not a universal gift. The gift is to be valued only as it is of use to the community: **But if there is no one to interpret, let them be silent in church** (14:28).

'God is really among you'

Whilst 'arguments from silence' are very open to error, it is interesting to consider what Paul does *not* say in these chapters on charismatic gifts and order in Christian worship. He does not say, 'But if there is no one to interpret, let *the elders of the church* tell those who speak in tongues to be silent' (cf. 14:28); or, 'If anyone speaks in a tongue, let *the leader of the congregation* choose two or at most three to speak in turn and choose one to interpret' (cf. 14:29). The instruction is first to the individuals who are seen as in some way autonomous, and certainly in control of their own speech or silence. It is also to the community corporately: **When you come together ... [l]et all things be done for building up** (14:26). As in his exhortations about the Lord's Supper (11:17–34), there is no mention of any elders or overseers to whom Paul appeals to shepherd the community into doing things **decently and in order**. Is this because there was then no such structure of appointed leaders? Or because whatever appointed leaders there were, it was not the acts of worship that they were appointed to lead? Or because Paul is addressing the whole community now and will have other private things to write to the leaders? Later letters in the Pauline tradition, 1 and 2 Timothy and Titus, are apparently addressed to individual shepherds of the Church.

The recognition of widespread charismatic gifts and the appointment of church officers are not necessarily mutually exclusive arrangements. We do, however, need to read this letter without assuming the formalised practices of the later Church where charismatic gifts do not remain the basis and focus of ministry. The questions need to be brought together with other issues of equality and authority that we have explored in the letter. While there seem to have been appointed ministries for some people, these can have varied and imprecise titles or descriptions, and there was room for dispute about the nature or scope of some people's authority. The operation of the Spirit in the community was especially an issue in public worship, where Paul does not refer to appointed officers.

Reflecting on the message and the method

If we are members of Christian communities ourselves, we may need to release Paul from the burden of supplying a ready-made blueprint for a ministry that our own churches might need. There were some (many) questions that Paul was *not* trying to answer. Paul's eschatological urgency (e.g. 1 Cor. 7:29) suggests that a long-term structuring of church leadership was not in view. The principles Paul is working with on the matter of public worship were applied to one situation in Corinth: how far do they reproduce the same pattern of worship when applied to a different situation?

In Corinth, there seem to have been differences in perceived status between different functions, based on conspicuous spiritual endowment and social superiority. The rich, educated and socially influential may have been the leaders of opinion in the congregation, and may have led in worship too. This would have been a real problem for the unity of the congregation – countered by Paul's theology of different functions as gifts from the same Spirit.

Paul's theology of charismatic gifts is not a draft for church officers – his purpose is anti-enthusiastic to avoid pride and dominance, and to encourage all Christians to use gifts in mutual submission and edification of the whole church.

Leaders, of whatever sort, with the entire congregation are in a context of co-operation and love – and love **does not insist on its own way**. It was the task of each to participate in worship for the building up of the community and for the common good. The functions that Paul notes are more important than the status of those exercising the functions. The roles represent gifts of the Spirit and appointment by God.

Paul's use of the body metaphor in 1 Corinthians 12 and his description of the operation of love in 13 are explicitly antihierarchical. Paul's criterion of rank – and of the greater gifts – is governed by the idea of the **common good**: all should work for this, and honour all the members of the community.

✏️   How far are you convinced by the arguments that Paul's churches, like the one at Corinth, were not governed in worship by a formal leadership?

What other features of Pauline theology support or counter this representation? Can you point to texts in 1 Corinthians or elsewhere in Paul to support your evaluation?

If this was an early pattern, why does a different, formalised and hierarchical pattern develop in most or all of the churches later?

Suggestions for further reading

Banks, Robert, 1980. *Paul's Idea of Community: the early house churches in their historical setting*, Exeter, Paternoster Press, pp. 131–51

Dunn, James D.G., 1995. *1 Corinthians: New Testament Guides*, Sheffield, Sheffield Academic Press, pp. 79–84

Ellis, E. Earle, 1989. *Pauline Theology: ministry and society*, Exeter, Paternoster Press, pp. 87–121

Frör, Hans, 1995. *YouWretched Corinthians!: the correspondence between the Church in Corinth and Paul,* trans. J. Bowden, London, SCM, pp. 62–72

Hill, Edmund, OP, 1988. *Ministry and Authority in the Catholic Church*, London, Geoffrey Chapman, pp. 26–31

Jansen, John F., 1993. 'Glossolalia', in B.M. Metzger *et al.* (eds.), *The Oxford Companion to the Bible*, Oxford, OUP, p. 255

Stott, John, 2002. *Calling Christian Leaders: biblical models of church, gospel and ministry*, Leicester, IVP

Witherington, Ben, 1995. *Conflict and Community in Corinth: socio-rhetorical commentary on 1 and 2 Corinthians*, Carlisle, Paternoster Press, pp. 253–90

In this chapter, reference was also made to the following works

Gillespie, Thomas, 1994. *The First Theologians*, Grand Rapids, Eerdmans

MacDonald, Margaret Y., 1988. *The Pauline Churches: a socio-historical study of institutionalisation in the Pauline and Deutero-Pauline writings*, Cambridge, CUP

Stendahl, K., 1977. 'Glossolalia – the New Testament Evidence', in *Paul Among Jews and Gentiles, and other essays*, London, SCM

Theissen, Gerd, 1987. *Psychological Aspect of Pauline Theology*, Edinburgh, T&T Clark

Thiselton, A.C., 2000. *First Epistle to the Corinthians*, Carlisle, Paternoster Press

CHAPTER 9

'Authority on her head': women's freedom or constraints in worship

1 Corinthians 11:2–16 and 14:26–40

In the two previous chapters, we looked at Paul's teaching to women and men about marriage and to the whole community about worship. The two issues come together in the passages to which we now turn. They are at the beginning and the end of the section of the letter (1 Cor. 11–14) in which Paul addresses issues in worship. In dealing with these, the letter refers twice to distinctions concerning women and men. As in the teaching on marriage in chapter 7, Paul is concerned for good order. At the same time Christian freedom – which was probably part of Paul's original teaching in Corinth (Hurd 1965, p. 287) – may be central to the issues.

Decently and in order

If you attend Christian worship, how far do you expect it to reflect the contemporary culture around you, and how far do you see it as a tradition which stands apart from a secular culture? Are the ministers dressed as other people are outside the church, or robed in clothes that reflect a separate tradition? Do the members of the congregation behave much as they do in the rest of their lives or do they adopt different postures and sing to a different kind of music?

There may be a tension between a liturgical tradition and contemporary culture in many or all types of church worship. Amplified bands playing loud music in a contemporary fashion, young people in baseball caps and a minister with a pierced eyebrow can seem to traditionally minded worshippers to be discourteous to their feelings or even irreligious in some broader way. Conversely, robed ministers, organ music and archaic language may seem like dinosaur-land to some of those same young people.

Something was happening in the Corinthian congregation that may have reflected and resembled or challenged cultural expression outside the church. There may have been a similar tension to those described above, between worshippers who felt free to behave in public worship in a way that seemed inappropriate to Paul and perhaps to others in the congregation. The tensions I described in British Christian and secular culture were, broadly, generational. In Corinth, it was the perception of gender, and appropriate, distinctive behaviour of women and men in the culture, that seems to have occasioned a difference of view and practice.

Any man/woman who prays or prophesies

Our first passage is 1 Corinthians 11:2–16, and we will take the verses slightly out of order. We will try to start with what the situation in Corinth appears to be, examine the heart of Paul's argument, then the related arguments and finally the additional arguments he adds which may not be wholly integral to the main argument.

📖   Reread I Corinthians 11:4–6.

Who is doing what in the community's worship, and why might they be doing so?

It is difficult to be certain about quite what custom Paul is criticising and what custom he wishes to establish in 11:2–16. The traditional conjecture is that Paul was insisting that women praying and prophesying in community worship should wear the veil according to Jewish custom, as against a Greek custom of women speaking in public unveiled. However, there is no noun in the Greek text here that means 'veil'. The meaning is carried in a verb which means 'to cover'.

We ought to take seriously the charge that we may be too readily assuming (and why is that?) that the people at fault are some women in Corinth, rather than assuming that Paul may be reprimanding men for something *they* are doing. Verse 4 of chapter 11 suggests the latter possibility. Richard Oster has argued, for instance, that the problem in Corinth was that male believers had taken to the practice of wearing head-coverings during prayer. If this is so, they would have been reflecting a Roman devotional ethos (1988, pp. 483, 505).

Married Roman women in public customarily wore their hair up and a hood over their heads (as on the medallion on the cover illustration of this book). The explanation in 11:15 suggests that at least one of the issues is how women wore their hair when leading ecstatic worship, and that some (or even one?) of the Corinthian women let their hair flow freely instead of keeping it in the customary coiffure (Hurley 1981, pp. 168–71) and covered. Fiorenza suggests that the Corinthian women took on this custom by analogy to the worship of Isis, because Isis was also said to have made the power of women equal to men, and Isis' associations – like the Christian communities – admitted women and slaves to equal membership and active participation (1987, pp. 227–8). In opposition, Paul would be holding that ecstatic behaviour and unintelligible prayer did not submit to the corporate needs – to build up the community and to proclaim the gospel of Christ. (This aspect matches the teaching we saw in 1 Corinthians 12 and 14.)

The English phrase 'letting your hair down' carries a similar frame of reference and reflects the idea that to have your hair bound up is (or represents) a restraint on your behaviour, while letting long hair flow loose is a sensation (and an expression) of being unconfined, free. This might suggest that it would not be merely an association with other cultic worship, such as that of Isis, that inspired the women of Corinth to let their hair be unbound while they were participating in worship. They believed that spiritually they were 'free': Paul had taught them that they were (cf. 1 Cor. 9:1). In this respect, Paul's exhortation about the practice might match the question of eating food offered to idols: **'All things are lawful', but not all things build up** (10:23). Moreover, through Paul they had learned that **there is no longer male and female . . . in Christ Jesus** (Gal. 3:28). If their role in patriarchal marriage was not determinant for them in their participation in Christian community, then the social behaviour and appearance that usually marked out an adult woman from an unmarried girl, or from a sexually available woman, was not, they may have argued, essential or even desirable when they prayed or prophesied.

The theology then may have come from Paul. The application of the theology he seems not to have anticipated: this is from the Corinthian believers themselves. Antoinette Wire (1990) argues that 1 Corinthians in a large measure represents a conflict between Paul's apostolic authority and the prophetic autonomy of the Corinthian believers, mostly women. As we have seen these are not necessarily two different types of authority and Paul's own gospel would have encouraged a 'prophetic autonomy' – but under Christ, and therefore subject to the needs of the community.

The image and reflection of God

📖   Reread I Corinthians 11:7.

How much of this idea can you find in Genesis 1:26–7?

We almost certainly need to know something about the Jewish tradition that is influencing what Paul writes here. In the story of humankind's creation, we are told that God said, 'Let us make humankind in our image, according to our likeness . . . So God created humankind in his image . . . male and female he created them' (Gen. 1:26–7). A tradition of Jewish exegesis of this passage in Paul's time recognised that both male and female were created in the image of God (Gen. 1:27) but held that the 'likeness' of God was given to the male and not the female. This 'likeness' was seen in terms of 'reflection' or 'glory': as if the radiance of God shines off the face of God's creature. The female, this tradition holds, is in the *image* of God but does not directly reflect God's 'likeness' or 'glory'. Instead, because she derives from the male (interpreting Gen. 2:21–3), she reflects *his* 'likeness' or 'glory'. When we are aware of this tradition, it seems inescapable that Paul's argument here is influenced by it: 'For a man . . . is the image and reflection [Greek, *doxa*: glory] of God; but woman is the reflection [*doxa*] of man.' In this view, if a man covered his head he failed to reflect God's glory: therefore in worship he should not cover his head. If a woman covered her head, she ceased to reflect the glory of her man, her husband, and in worship she should not reflect her husband's glory. The idea seems to be that with a covered head, hiding this derived and secondary glory, she is free to reflect her Creator's own glory.

Here is Morna Hooker's analysis which opened up this interpretation:

> In Jewish thought the *doxa* given to Adam was closely connected with his creation in the *eikōn theou* [image of God] and

with his authority over the rest of creation: although Gen.
1:26f. speaks of this authority being given to both male and
female, Jewish exegesis did not in fact allow it to Eve, and with
this view Paul is clearly in agreement. Yet now woman, too,
speaks to God in prayer and declares his word in prophecy: to
do this she needs authority and power from God. The head-covering which symbolizes the effacement of man's glory in the
presence of God also serves as a sign of the *exousia* [authority]
which is given to the woman; with the glory of man hidden she,
too, may reflect the glory of God. Far from being a symbol of
the woman's subjection to man, therefore, her head-covering is
what Paul calls it – authority: in prayer and prophecy she,
like the man, is under the authority of God. Although the
differences of creation remain, and are reflected in the difference of dress, it is nevertheless true that in relation to God
'there is neither male nor female; for you are all one in Christ
Jesus'. (1990, pp. 119–20)

If we ourselves do not interpret the creation story in Genesis as Paul
seems to here, we may well find the reasoning behind his exhortation
unconvincing. Hooker's analysis, however, and the influence of this
Jewish exegesis of Genesis, may help us with Paul's other apparent
references to Genesis in the passage to which we turn now.

All things come from God

Reread I Corinthians 11:3 and 11:8–12.

Can you trace any references to Genesis 2 in these verses?

In 11:3 there are two issues of translation we need to bear in mind.
One is (as noted above in Chapter 7) that the Greek words for **man**
and **woman** are also used for **husband** and **wife**. It is the relationship of 'male and female' in the context of the Genesis narrative,
where the context is their union and procreation (i.e. marriage), that
is key to this verse. The other Greek word to consider is *kephalē*,
which means **head**. The use of this word in Paul's argument is
surely influenced by the matter in hand: that what men and women
are or are not putting on their physical *heads* is the issue. However,
several scholars have argued that *kephalē*, as in the English phrase 'the

head of the river', can also mean 'source'. The idea is disputed but it makes the connection that the authority or headship of a husband over his wife derives from the idea in Genesis 2:23: 'she shall be called Woman [Hebrew, *ishshah*] because she was taken out of Man [Hebrew, *ish*].' This seems to be confirmed by 11:8: **Indeed, man was not made from woman, but woman from man.**

There is a chiastic pattern in 11:8–12 which means that Paul almost corrects himself in the matter of women's subordination. (A chiasm is a pattern of writing or speech where matching or parallel clauses are put first in one order, *a* then *b*, and then the order is reversed, *b* then *a*.) In chapter 11 verse 8 is matched or countered by verse 12, and verse 9 by verse 11, and these frame verse 10. The idea (from Genesis) in 11:3 and 11:8 that a man is the source of a woman is balanced by the recognition (from biology and experience) that a woman, a mother, is the source of a man.

> a. Indeed, man was not made from woman, but woman from man (11:8).
> a. For just as woman came from man, so man comes through woman (11:12).

The teaching from Genesis that it was for the man's sake that the woman was brought into being is likewise countered by the inter-dependence of men and women in Christ.

> b. Neither was man created for the sake of woman, but woman for the sake of man (11:9).
> b. Nevertheless, in the Lord woman is not independent (Greek, *chōris*) of man or man independent of woman (11:11).

There is yet another issue of translation in 11:11. Josef Kürzinger argues that *chōris* usually means not 'without' (and thus 'independent of') but 'different from' (1978, pp. 270–5). This means we might translate 11:11, **In the Lord woman is not different from man nor man different from woman**. This conforms to the baptismal formula of Galatians 3:28, **In Christ . . . there is no longer male and female**. Paul's argument thus counters the old order of creation with the new order of salvation. It leaves the question: how far should differences which might exist on the basis of nature and creation be present in the worship assembly of Christians?

Before he balances these clauses, Paul says it is **for this reason**, that is, resting on the pattern in Genesis, that a woman should cover her head in worship.

There is a tradition of interpreting 11:10 as saying that **a woman ought to have** 'a veil' **on her head** (e.g. RSV). The Greek text gives *exousia* (authority, power, freedom). By substituting 'veil' for authority, interpreters were identifying the *exousia* as that of a woman's husband: when she prays, she should demonstrate that she remains under her husband's authority. Their view was (is) that the head-covering is not a symbol of a woman's authority but of a wife's hierarchical subjection. This would be counter to the idea that in Christ a woman is not defined by her marriage: **there is no longer male and female** (Gal. 3:28). The text says **a woman ought to have authority on her head**. Morna Hooker's analysis above suggests that this is exactly what Paul means. By ceasing to reflect her husband's 'glory' she demonstrates that her authority to pray and prophesy is drawn from God and reflects God's glory.

Any interpretation raises the difficulty of the application of any such teaching to women who were not married, and to those whose husbands were not 'in Christ'. The focus is probably on married couples within the congregation.

📁 GLOSSARY : *The Angels*

There are four references to angels in 1 Corinthians (4:9; 6:3; 11:10; 13:1). The Greek, *Aggelos*, means 'messenger'. God's heavenly assistants in the Hebrew Bible have a number of functions but the term 'messenger' (Hebrew, *mal'āk*) became in time the word used to describe them all (Meier 1993, p. 27). One of their roles in Jewish thought is as watchers over the rest of the created order, which is the frame of reference for 1 Corinthians 4:9.

They are not divine (in the sense of being gods) in Jewish theology.

This is why Paul says, 'Do you not know that we are to judge angels?' (1 Cor. 6:3). Angels are part of the created order and, in the eschatological order under the Lordship of Christ, those who are 'in Christ' participate in Christ's sovereignty over the rest of creation.

The reference to the angels in 11:10 is one way or another a concern for order. 'Order' is an important factor in Paul's theology: in biblical traditions 'chaos' signifies the absence of God's presence or the Spirit's activity. Paul would have found it hard to associate anything that looked chaotic with the Spirit's motivation.

The reference to the angels in 11:10 could reflect the same role as in 4:9: they are watchers over the created order and will regard the women's uncovered heads as a 'lapse' from the right distinctions between the sexes in the *order* of creation. Angels were also held to be watchers over worship and liturgical order: here, Paul might be saying, angels would regard this ecstatic behaviour of the women as disorderly in terms of right worship.

Angels were also regarded as the mediators of words of prophecy. In 11:10, this might relate to the requirement for women to demonstrate, in a way appropriate to their sex, their authority to prophesy. This explanation takes seriously the *exousia*, the freedom or spiritual authority, of the women. The other explanations about order in creation or worship seem to suggest that the angels would be like those *outside* the church who misread the unbound or uncovered heads of the women as something other than an expression of their eschatological freedom. Angels, one might speculate, should be aware of God's new order.

The other biblical reference to 'angels' beholding women is about the 'sons of God' who saw the 'daughters of humans' in Genesis 6:1–4, and coupled with them. This may not be in Paul's mind at all, but it may share with an element of this situation the androcentric and patriarchal prescription that it behoves women to dress modestly lest they distract or attract males.

Judge for yourselves

📖 Reread 1 Corinthians 11:13–16.

Are these *new* reasons for exhorting women to cover their heads in worship rather than ones which relate to the argument made so far?

Who is to decide in this matter, and what influences does Paul think they should take into account?

This is the second time Paul has used the full phrase, **Judge for yourselves.** Here it introduces an additional argument to the one made so far based on a particular reading of Genesis. It uses terms like proper, nature, and degrading, and might reflect the cultural importance of 'shame' and 'honour' in Roman society but also the concern Paul expresses for decency and **order** (1 Cor. 14:40). It relates to some of the terms (e.g. **disgrace**) used in 11:4–6. He clearly associates some distinctions of dress and hairstyle between men and women with appropriate behaviour. If these distinctions have a general cultural currency, abandoning them may seem attention seeking or disruptive.

The arguments given in 11:14–15 are declaredly from **nature** but in fact they are from custom and culture. Paul's cultural environment accustomed him (and everyone else) to the idea that men wore their hair short and women wore their hair long, and that to diverge from either was to do something perverse (or foreign). It is a vivid instance of an exhortation in a biblical text deriving (in part) from the particulars of historical context. Paul's injunction draws on the culture of his correspondents: he expects them to react to unconventional behaviour in the same way that he does. If we do not share his cultural conditioning, it may be hard to see the force of the argument. Conformity to the expectations of society can have a moral force (as a courtesy to people with these expectations), but in a situational, temporal way rather than one which is universal and for all time. Moreover, some cultural conventions need to be challenged: perhaps the women prophets at Corinth thought so too.

There is a further slight shift of ground too. The last verse (11:16) forms an *inclusio* (a literary and rhetorical way of framing a passage, holding together the beginning and the end) with the sentence that introduced the subject. In 11:2 Paul commends the believers because, he says, **you remember me** and **maintain the traditions**. In 11:16, in something of a withdrawal of the Corinthians' right to **judge for** [them]**selves**, he refers them again to the traditions shared by all the **churches**, and encouraged by Paul himself (**we**). Remember how the opening of the letter hinted at possible idiosyncrasies of this community (1:2). The conditional clause, **if anyone is disposed to be contentious**, suggests Paul expected some opposition in this matter, and even that he felt his arguments were unlikely to have been convincing.

If there is no one to interpret, let them be silent

Before we examine the second passage in the letter that relates to wives and husbands in worship, we should remind ourselves of the context in which it comes in 1 Corinthians 14 (discussed in the previous chapter).

📖   Reread I Corinthians 14:26–33.

What reasons does Paul give here for exhorting some worshippers sometimes to be silent?

They should be subordinate

There is quite a large body of commentators who believe that some of these verses are an interpolation, not written by Paul, and indeed some of the ancient manuscripts, finding perhaps that they seem to interrupt the theme and flow of the passage, move 14:14, 33b–6 to the end of the chapter. Arguments for them being interpolated include their apparent contradiction of 1 Corinthians 11:2–16, and some use of words and phrases uncharacteristic of Paul (see, e.g., Senft and Schrage in Thiselton 2000, p. 1150). However, we shall wrestle with them to see if they do fit our understanding of Paul's teaching.

📖   Reread I Corinthians 14:34–6.

What are the indications that this passage is an interruption of the rest? Conversely, are there signs that it does fit in with its context?

More than ever here we might be struggling because we are only hearing, as it were, one end of the telephone conversation. Paul's correspondents may have addressed particular questions to him about specific individuals, specific practices, and his reply may use some words and phrases which reflect that context, but whose meaning appears more general when we read it without knowing that context.

The verses do have a literary context for us though. First, they are part of a letter in which Paul was at pains to describe (11:2–16) in rather a convoluted argument what he thought were the right conditions in which women should indeed pray and prophesy aloud in the congregation. If he thought they should all, at all times, remain silent, he could have saved himself, and us, a lot of trouble by saying so straight away!

Second, these verses follow others in which, for the **building up** of the whole community (14:26), glossalists are given guidelines on when to **be silent** (14:28 and 30). The context therefore suggests that what Paul writes about here is an instance of the same sort of circumstance: the self-regulation (by all the members) of order in worship. Again if we assume that only the women are, or one woman is, at fault, we are probably missing the implications: whatever the problem is, the solution involves a married couple talking together **at home** (14:35) so the matter is not about Christian women with pagan husbands, but Christian couples, or even a single Christian couple in the community. Remember again that the Greek text does not distinguish between **wives** and **women**.

Earl Ellis suggests that the circumstance might be an instance of what Paul describes in 14:29: **Let two or three prophets speak, and let the others weigh what is said**. If one of the people making prophetic utterance was a married man, and one of those with a gift of discernment or interpretation was his wife (12:10), her co-participation in worship with him might involve her publicly **weighing** or testing (14:29) her husband's message (1981, p. 218). Whilst we may not think this is intrinsically a problem, we can probably all think of married couples whose public disagreements make us think, 'I wish they would do this at home . . .'

Part of the theological context in which we should read the text is the one we have pursued throughout the letter: that Paul teaches a voluntary subordination of each to each, after the pattern of Christ crucified, for the building up of the whole Body. If Ellis is right, then the subordination enjoined on the women is not necessarily an old order social stratification where wives must merely obey their husbands. The text of 14:34 does not include a superordinate: it does not say, for example, they must be subordinate 'to their husbands'. Like the glossalists in 14:28, what they should voluntarily subordinate themselves to is the needs of the whole community.

This is not how the passage has traditionally been interpreted. In a study of the word 'subordinate', Delling writes of this instance: 'it simply denotes the status of women as such' (1972, p. 43), that is, a hierarchical stratification of **male and female** like that of the contemporary secular society and not as **in Christ**.

Although this subordination for the needs of others may be similar to that of the glossalists, this injunction is gender-specific. It is the woman of the couple who must be silent and ask her husband **at home**. The attribution of **shame** to her action (14:35) and the argument that **the law** also enjoins this (14:34) all seem to belong to the social stratification outside the church. This is not in the Torah, so the appeal to **the law** may represent assimilation of Greco-Roman injunctions on wives into Jewish-Hellenistic missionary tradition. This argument from 'law' seems uncharacteristic of Paul and is part of the evidence offered by those who see the verses as a non-Pauline interpolation.

As in 11:2 and 16, there is an *inclusio* relating the practice to what happens in **all the churches**. So Paul frames the passage by calling on them to recognise the practice of the other churches and recognise their unity with them (14:33, 36).

How far Paul's teaching here respects the eschatological freedom and authority of the married women believers and how far this is shaped or curtailed by his view of the distinctions of the sexes in nature or culture we will return to in our reflection on his message and the method below.

A command of the Lord

📖   Reread I Corinthians 14:37–40.

Is there a tension between Paul's authoritative command here, and the 'dialectic authority' of persuasion and exhortation to Judge for yourselves?

The rhetoric of these final verses on order in worship suggests some expectation of *resistance* from his correspondents to a self-regulation that these wives, or this wife, should keep silence in community worship (in the particular circumstances under discussion). It is possible that Paul does not expect his exhortation to be accepted without protest by the Corinthian community – where, after all, women and wives were known to have place among leading apostles and missionaries. We remember too that passages in 2 Corinthians suggest that the Corinthians did not accept Paul's teaching (about something) at this point in their relationship.

The rejection of the *reality* of the **spiritual powers** of those who disagree with him is, surely, a disempowering statement (Wire 1990, pp. 14–17). I have argued that Paul's method on the whole is an empowering one, but it does embrace this claim to an authority by which the believers should weigh their own. His final sentence (14:39–40) is a fascinating balance of his encouragement of *their* spiritual authority and the corporate (and external) necessity for decency and **order**.

Reflecting on the message and the method

In the matter of eating food offered to idols, Paul had written, **Give no offence to Jews or to Greeks or to the church of God** (10:32). Although the proclamation of Christ crucified was itself *offensive* (1:23), Paul encourages the church to **try to please everyone in everything** they do (10:33).

His injunctions to the women prophets to cover their heads, and to consult their husbands at home rather than dispute with them in public worship, can be seen as part of the ethics of the cross: a voluntary constraint of rights and freedom for the benefit of others, like the other examples of this we have seen.

However, the fact that the women should dress in a way that conforms to a cultural constraint of women in relation to men (11:2–16), and should **ask their husbands at home** if **they desire to know** anything (14:35), is a shaping of the principle of mutual and voluntary submission in the pattern of patriarchy, which expresses an *in*voluntary and *not*-mutual subordination of women to men. At the very least, Paul is 'quietist' here in his ethics, in a conformity with the status quo of a stratified society. This contrasts with the instances we have seen (for example, concerning the Lord's Supper, and food offered to idols) where the exhortation *reverses* accepted social stratification and encourages the submission of the higher to the lower (measured by economic and social status).

On the whole it is decency and order within the congregation that seems to concern him about this issue, more than any charge of impropriety from those outside the church, ignorant of the eschatological order. Nevertheless the social status of women outside the community seems to inhibit in his view the freedom Christian women could exercise inside.

✎ How convincing do you find Paul's argument (11:2–16) for a woman's prophetic authority being marked out by a particular, gender-specific, cultural practice?

✎   How far does the *reversal* of social stratifications (e.g. of the rich who **wait** for the poor, 11:33) apply to the subordination of wives to husbands?

Suggestions for further reading

Allison, R., 1988. 'Let Women be Silent in Churches. 1 Cor 14.33b–36 – What did Paul say, What did he really mean?', *Journal for the Study of the New Testament*, 32, 27–40

Ellis, E. Earle, 1981. 'The Silenced Wives of Corinth' in Epp and Fee (eds.), *New Testament Textual Criticism*, Oxford, OUP

Hall, David, 1990. 'A Problem of Authority', *Expository Times*, 102, 2, 39–42

Hooker, M.D., 1963–4. 'Authority on her Head', *New Testament Studies*, 10, 415–6

. . . 1990. 'Authority on her head' in *From Adam to Christ*, Cambridge, CUP, pp. 119–20

Whelan, Caroline, 1993. '*Amica Pauli*: the role of Phoebe in the Early Church', *Journal for the Study of the New Testament*, 49, 67–85

Wire, A.C., 1990. *The Corinthian Women Prophets*, Minneapolis, Fortress

In this chapter, reference was also made to the following works

Delling, G., 1972. 'Hupotassein' in *Theological Dictionary of the New Testament*, ed. Kittel and Friedrich, 9 vols. (1964–74) VIII, pp. 39–46

Fiorenza, E. Schüssler, 1983. *In Memory of Her: a feminist theological reconstruction of Christian origins*, London, SCM

Hurd, J.C., 1965. *The Origin of 1 Corinthians*, London, SPCK

Hurley, J.B., 1981. *Man and Woman in Biblical Perspective*, Leicester

Kürzinger, J., 1978. 'Frau und Mann nach 1 Kor 11.11f', *Biblische Zeitschrift*, 22, 270–5

Meier, Samuel A., 1993. In B.M. Metzger *et al.* (eds.), *The Oxford Companion to the Bible*, Oxford, OUP, pp. 27–8

Oster, R.E., 1988. 'When Men wore Veils to Worship', *New Testament Studies*, 34, pp. 483–505

Thiselton, A.C., 2000. *The First Epistle to the Corinthians* Carlisle, Paternoster Press

CHAPTER 10

'If you can gain your freedom': slaves and the hierarchical household

1 Corinthians 7:17–24 (and 1 Timothy 5:3–16)

We have seen that domestic relationships between wives and husbands have some impact on Paul's ideas about Christian relationships. In this chapter we consider the idea that the 'household' became an influential model for the way the church developed, as well as looking at another domestic relationship: that between slaves and their owners. This will lead us to make connections between the reality of slavery and Paul's theology (eschatology and Christology) of freedom. We will then take a further look at wives and husbands in the developing church.

Affairs of the world

The influence of our domestic situation, of home and family, is often appealed to as the formative one for matters of morals and social behaviour. By a person's 'background', we often mean 'what their home circumstances were like as they grew up'. We are not tied to them: we may throw off or revise the habits, the lifestyle, or the ethics of the homes we come from. They are formative but not definitive.

The conventions of homes and households have been far from static in different times and different cultures, and 'family values' would have meant different things in the polygamous tents of Abraham, the slave-run house of Philemon or, possibly, in the room above the shop of Prisca and Aquila. Clearly there is some continuity in the domestic roles of women in Britain today with their counterparts of other times, but also much change and potential for change. Now, many of us might feel uncomfortable were we to be served by house-servants at a friend's house, let alone (and 'uncomfortable' would not be the word) by house-slaves. Children's roles too have undergone great change: the idea that they have 'rights', must not be beaten, and that their choices are upheld in courts of law, would have deeply bewildered some parents, not a hundred years ago.

Households reflect their cultural context. The ethos of family homes may also influence the culture. ('And the hand that rocks the cradle, Is the hand that rules the world . . .': William Ross Wallace, 1819–81.)

Bought with a price

Slaves were not necessarily at the bottom of the social scale, or of all social scales; some slaves of high 'status-dissonance' had wealth, prestige, professional or clerical skills as secretaries and managers entrusted with enormous power, opportunity and even, effectively, slaves of their own. Conversely, there were free labourers who starved. There were also, of course, slaves in menial drudgery over whom their owners had arbitrary power of humiliation, torture and death. Recent research on slavery in the Roman Empire suggests that the nature of slavery depended fundamentally on *to whom* one was enslaved (Combes 1998, pp. 49–67, 77–94) and this links us back – Chapter 3 above – to Paul's use of Lord for Jesus. Nevertheless, socially, the threshold between the slave and free remained funda-mental to a perception of a person's place in household and society.

There were both slaves and slave-owners among the Pauline Christians, though the ethos of the leaders is clearly that of the owners rather than the slaves. It is very likely that freedwomen and freedmen, however, are to be found among congregation leaders as well as among the membership. Although we cannot know whether or not the bishop Onesimus in Ephesus in 110 CE was the slave we read about in the Letter to Philemon, his name indicates that he was or had been a slave, and now was an overseer in a Pauline Christian community.

Just as the eschatological freedom of Christians led to conflict over the social liberties of Christian women, so slaves must have been inspired with the expectation of a change in status.

Were you a slave when called?

Reread I Corinthians 7:17–24.

Remind yourself of the context of this parenthetic example (discussed in Chapter 7) and of its relationship to the confessional statement cited in Galatians 3:28.

There is an extraordinary example of a translation problem in 1 Corinthians 7:21. In this instance it is not a difficulty with the manuscript traditions, or with the vocabulary: it is that the Greek here is wholly ambiguous. The first half is unproblematic (in terms of translation at least):

> Were you a slave when called? Do not be concerned about it.

A very literal translation of the second half gives us this:

> But if (or, even if) you may become free, prefer to use [it].

Compare these two translations:

Revised Standard:	Were you a slave when called? Never mind. But if you can gain your freedom, avail yourself of the opportunity.
New International:	Were you a slave when you were called? Don't let it trouble you – although if you can gain your freedom, do so.

with these two:

New Jerusalem:	So, if when you were called, you were a slave, do not think it matters – even if you have a chance of freedom, you should prefer to make full use of your condition as a slave.
New Revised Standard:	Were you a slave when called? Do not be concerned about it. Even if you can gain your freedom, make use of your present condition now more than ever.

The key differences hinge on two words: *mallon chrēsai*. These mean 'rather use [it]', or 'prefer to use [it]'. The problem is that the 'it' is inferred. Does Paul mean, 'Prefer to use [that opportunity for freedom]' or, 'Prefer to use [your present condition as a slave]'? The RSV and NIV plump for the former, and the NJB and NRSV conclude it means the latter. We can reproduce the ambiguity of the Greek in English if we make a very literal translation,

as the King James tends to be, and leave open what 'it' refers to:
e.g.

> King James   Art thou called *being* a servant? care not for it:
> Version: but if thou mayest be made free, use *it* rather.

Use *what* rather? The hermeneutical circle guides us to try to interpret this part in relation to its context in this letter and in Paul's
theology, but we might still have to live with the ambiguity. **Do not
become slaves of human masters** (7:23) suggests that slaves are
to opt for freedom, legal as well as spiritual (as RSV and NIV). However 7:20 (cf. 7:17 and 7:24), **Let each of you remain in the
condition in which you were called**, suggests they should *not*
seek to change their status (as NRSV and NJB).

Paul doesn't appear to be addressing issues of slavery or circum-
cision in this passage in other than a secondary and illustrative way,
though it is hard to imagine the slaves in the Corinthian community
thinking the matter secondary. Paul is silent on the ethics of slavery
as an *institution* – unlike some Stoics of his time, like Seneca, who
articulate some humane ideals. Paul's silence on this may be because
of the nearness of the end, the insignificance of Christians as a
political force or because it genuinely did not occur to him. Fiorenza
notes that Paul's contribution is only one part of the dialogue: 'the
theological counterarguments by slaves and women have not
survived in history . . .' (1983, p. 217).

Slave of Christ

Does Paul's theology help us see which he might have intended? The
whole issue must be related to Paul's eschatological perspective. Both
his sense of the imminence of the end and of the already-realised conditions of the end lead him to his **opinion** that it is **well . . . to
remain as you are** (7:25–6). This is both **in view of the
impending crisis** (7:26), and because freedom in Christ was
already theirs: **Already you have all you want** (4:8).

He uses the language of captivity and freedom, lordship and service throughout his letters. He uses slavery in his metaphors of salvation (see Martin 1990): for Paul, the world is subject to the dominion
of other powers, and of sin and death (e.g. 1 Cor. 15:24; Rom. 8:38;
Gal. 1:4); in Christ, **creation itself will be set free from its**

bondage to decay and will obtain the freedom of the glory of the children of God (Rom. 8:21). Paradoxically, this means being subject to God in Christ, and under his dominion – though this is a subordination of free consent and the saving grace is a free gift.

We saw Paul's repeated reference to himself as **prisoner of Christ Jesus** in Philemon. The key language of voluntary subjection or subordination in 1 Corinthians 15:28 is related to the pattern of Christ's servanthood and his lordship. In Galatians, Paul identifies Christian freedom with the ethics of being 'slaves to one another':

> For you were called to freedom, brothers and sisters; only do not use your freedom as an opportunity for self-indulgence, but through love become slaves to one another. (Gal. 5:13)

He characterises his own ministry in the same way:

> For though I am free with respect to all, I have made myself a slave to all. (1 Cor. 9:19)

So in our passage it is wholly in accord with this apparent paradox that Paul writes:

> For whoever was called in the Lord as a slave is a freed person belonging to the Lord, just as whoever was free when called is a slave of Christ. (1 Cor. 7:22)

Once again, the relationship of two fellow Christians who might otherwise claim authority one over another is put in the context of their common subjection to Christ (**slave or free**; **Jew or Greek**; **male and female**, Gal. 3:28). With slaves, the decisive thing for Paul was that they continue in *the calling to freedom* entered into at baptism, regardless of social status.

The church that meets in your house

The meeting places of the Pauline communities were private houses. If the Christian congregation adapted to the model of the 'household', this has implications both for their relationship to outside society and for their internal structure.

We have already seen that the customs of a household in food given to guests of different social status may have had an impact on how the Corinthian Christians kept **the Lord's Supper**. In that instance Paul insists that this kind of status-consciousness is inimical to the common life of the members of the Body of Christ. However, the involuntary subordination of a wife to her husband in the secular and patriarchal household is a status-consciousness, Paul implies, that is in some measure still applicable, in the new order under Christ, to the behaviour of women and men in Christian worship.

We recall that the Christian movement was neither wholly conformist nor wholly separatist. Within the larger society, it was a 'conflict movement' which stood in tension to the social order outside it. Paul's exhortations testify to the tensions between the Christian community and the institutions of slavery, social hierarchy and the patriarchal family. The Christian community did not withdraw from the rest of society as did other communities or cults where social hierarchies were rejected and women admitted in full membership. Freewomen, freemen and slaves were admitted to the Christian movement while they still continued to live with pagan spouses or in pagan households.

Wayne Meeks has argued that it was the influence of the household structure that set the stage for some conflicts about roles of different members in Christian community and the allocation of power. In a household, the head of the household (whose Latin title is *paterfamilias*, the 'father of the household') exercised considerable authority over the members of the household and had some legal responsibility for them.

> The structure of the *oikos* [household] was hierarchical, and contemporary political and moral thought regarded the structure of superior and inferior roles as basic to the well-being of the whole society. Yet . . . there were certain countervailing modes and centres of authority in the Christian movement that ran contrary to the power of the *paterfamilias*, and certain egalitarian beliefs and attitudes that conflicted with the hierarchical structure. (1983, p. 76)

Scholars are divided on the matter of egalitarian beliefs and hierarchical structure. Some (like Meeks here, and Fiorenza) see a pattern where early egalitarian beliefs in the church were later compromised and a hierarchy of power and status, matching secular values, was imposed or reasserted in the churches. For example (Meeks again):

In time, in circles that appealed to the memory of Paul as an authority, whether or not they stood in any concrete social continuity with the Pauline mission, the whole church would be construed as 'the household of God,' with great stress upon the hierarchical order of the various roles peculiar to the ecclesiastical organisation. (1983, p. 77)

Others, finding passages in the New Testament excluding women from roles in the church and exhorting obedience from slaves to their masters, deduce or assume a fairly uniform practice in the first-century churches of the Pauline mission.

In Pauline studies, the authorship of some letters is a related issue. Colossians and Ephesians differ a little in language, style and theology from the undisputed letters. One or both might be by Paul; or it might be that Paul gave a greater responsibility in one or both to the person actually writing the letter; or one or both might be pseudonymous, that is, written in Paul's name. Pseudonimity was not an unusual practice in the first century. There is nearly a consensus in scholarship that 1 and 2 Timothy and Titus (sometimes referred to as 'The Pastoral Letters') are not by Paul, and were probably written in the 80s. (For a summary of the arguments see, e.g., Karris 1993, p. 574.) The many non-Pauline words and concepts in these suggest a later author who wanted to apply Paul's teaching in new situations, in some continuity with Paul's own mission. The occasional personal notes might be fragments of genuine letters of Paul.

This is pertinent to our investigation because of the challenge to the assumption of a uniform practice in Pauline churches. Colossians and Ephesians each includes a version of the 'Household Code' (see below) and the Pastorals suggest a great desire to conform to society's standards with no challenge to patriarchy or social hierarchies.

⬭ GLOSSARY : *The Household Codes*

In later letters of the Pauline circle, Colossians and Ephesians, there are passages where instructions are given to three pairs of household members: to wives and husbands, children and parents, slaves and owners/masters (Col. 3:18–4:1; Eph. 5:21–6.9; cf. 1 Pet. 2:13–3:7). The passages have been given the name Household Codes (or, in

German, *Haustafeln*) by biblical commentators.

The basic pattern is this (from Col. 3:18–4:1):

Wives, be subject to your
    husbands ...
Husbands, love your wives ...
Children, obey your parents ...
Fathers, do not provoke your
    children ...
Slaves, obey your earthly
    masters ...
Masters, treat your slaves
    justly ...

A majority of scholars holds that these are an adaptation of Greco-Roman (e.g. Lohse 1971, pp. 154–7) or Jewish-Hellenistic (e.g. Crouch 1972, pp. 74–101) philosophical religious codes. Certainly, they reflect the pattern of the common rhetorical topic, 'on the ordering of the household' (Greek, *peri oikonomias*).

Our concern with the ethics of 1 Corinthians, an earlier and undisputed Pauline letter, leads us to ask how far the ethos of the *Haustafeln* is also a development of Paul's early teaching, within the Church, rather than something primarily adapted from pagan or Jewish sources.

In Colossians, the passage just before the *Haustafel* or Household Code, is a version of the formula we saw in Galatians 3:28, but the male and female pairing is omitted entirely:

In that renewal there is no longer Greek and Jew, circumcised and uncircumcised, barbarian, Scythian, slave and free; but Christ is all and in all! (Col. 3:11)

However, the Ephesians code opens with the universal injunction to all Christians to subordinate themselves to the needs of others. In fact, in the Greek there is no verb in the next clause exhorting wives to be subject to their husbands – the verb is inferred from the previous, universal injunction:

Be subject to one another out of reverence for Christ, wives ... to your husbands ... (Eph. 5:21–2)

The subordination of Christian wives is thus phrased as a particular example of the general rule. However, 'be subject' is never addressed *individually* to husbands, parents or slave-owners.

There is no doubt that these are letters of the Pauline circle, so if not by Paul they are by followers of Paul. It has been possible for him or them to preach the freedom of slaves in Christ, and the authority of women to pray and prophesy, and to remain free of marriage; and yet also he has or they have felt constrained by patriarchal and hierarchical social values to avoid statements that husbands should likewise be subject to their wives, fathers to their children, masters to their slaves.

In these codes, the Greco-Roman patriarchal pattern of marital relationships and household hierarchy is adopted as part of a 'Christian' social ethic. The Ephesians code actually *theologises* the social structures of unequal power: wives are to be subject to their husbands as they are 'to the Lord' (Eph. 5:22). This might seem a long step from the idea that 'the husband does not have authority over his own body, but his wife does' (I Cor. 7:4), but perhaps not such a long step from the quietism of 'let them ask their husbands at home' (I Cor. 14:35).

Let a widow be put on the list

Is it valid to read back teaching, such as that on hierarchy in household roles, in a reverse trajectory from post-Pauline or even later Pauline exhortation, and let this determine our reading of Paul's ethics in earlier letters? We should certainly consider the other trajectory: that is, that some time after the Corinthian correspondence, it was not impossible for churches of the Pauline mission to enshrine teaching such as, 'Wives, be subject to your husbands' (Col. 3:18), or 'I permit no woman to teach or have authority over a man' (1 Tim. 2:12), or 'Let all who are under the yoke of slavery regard their masters as worthy of all honour' (1 Tim. 6:1).

We will take one example from the Pastorals that, arguably, bears a direct relation to some teaching in 1 Corinthians.

Read 1 Timothy 5:3–16.

Look for the financial implications in this passage of recognising permanent widowhood.

The regularisation of widows with a permanent vocation to the non-married state is a fascinating insight into the long-term effects of a teaching Paul records in 1 Corinthians 7:39–40:

> A wife is bound as long as her husband lives. But if the husband dies, she is free to marry anyone she wishes, only in the Lord. But in my judgement she is more blessed if she remains as she is. And I think that I too have the Spirit of God.

It emerges from 1 Timothy 5 that a number of women had followed Paul's exhortation and chosen not to remarry after being widowed. Remember the social patterns that meant that women might be widowed at a young age, and that for them to choose in this way was an exercise of freedom contrary to social norms and to the authority of the *paterfamilias*. It also made the woman financially vulnerable. In a society where few women were economically independent or could earn enough to live on, she would normally have been the financial responsibility of her husband, and then on his death the responsibility of her paternal family.

The **list** in 1 Timothy appears to be a list of widows who are eligible for financial support from the Christian community, because they have chosen not to remarry. The author of 1 Timothy gives reasons from his experience or his prejudice, or both, to deny this position to women under sixty. He seems to think their vocation cannot be genuine or cannot last. However, it is also apparent that the church would find it hard to support all the women under sixty who might choose not to remarry and would need support (5:16). In particular, if the woman is from a believing household, she should be supported by members of her family (5:8).

In this regularisation of the lives of women in keeping with the patriarchy of the day, we have come a long way from Paul's **Remain in the condition in which you were called** (1 Cor. 7:20). And yet we are here largely because of that very teaching. Women had indeed claimed their freedom in Christ, but the church found it hard to accommodate their freedom.

Similarly we could relate passages like 1 Timothy 2:11–15 (with its – to my mind – misogynist reading of Genesis) to the teaching of 1 Corinthians 11:10 where a woman is to speak with **authority on her head**. You need not tell people to stop doing something if they are not doing it (and presumably believe they are free to do it). What the author of 1 Timothy tells us in requiring women to be silent is that Christian women *are* teaching and having **authority over** men and women in their community. They are doing so because Paul's teaching, surely, had guided them to do so.

Reflecting on the message and the method

The New Testament has collected together at least one text where women seem to exercise authority in public worship, and at least another where they are told they may not, and both of these bear the name of one author. This should make us very wary of assuming a uniform practice in the early churches, even in that tradition that owed something or much to Paul's practice and teaching.

The eighty-year or so span of the New Testament texts chart the forging of Christianity in a number of thoroughly related but significantly different forms. Some traditions may have been aware of their differences from others. The significant role that John's Gospel gives to the testimony and discipleship of women may reflect, in some measure, a conscious response in the Johannine community to the exclusion of women from ecclesial office in the (roughly contemporary) post-Pauline community that is reflected in the Pastorals. The Johannine community may in effect have been saying, 'What you are teaching is not how we understand the discipleship of women as we have learned it in the traditions about Jesus.'

Paul's reputation for misogyny is to an extent based on the understanding that he is the author of the Pastorals. Even when this is not the premise, it is often argued that the ecclesial hierarchy and patriarchy of the Pastorals reflects Paul's own patriarchalism. We are getting ourselves to the place where we can judge for ourselves whether this is so and whether we can hold together the baptismal vision of Galatians 3:28 and the injunctions of 1 Timothy.

Throughout our study of 1 Corinthians I have been attempting to apply Paul's proclamation of **Christ crucified**, and his conviction concerning the consummation of God's purposes in **the end**, to the various matters discussed between him and the Corinthians. The Christology and the eschatology are crucial to the acclamation in Galatians that **in Christ there is no longer slave or free**, **male and female**. Where is this Christology and eschatology in the later, post-Pauline letters? It seems to me a vindication of the focus we have held on these key, interlocking, elements of Paul's theology, applied to the situations of Christian subordination in 1 Corinthians, that where the ethics of subordination are different as they are in the Pastorals, this reflects the difference in the theology, and a shift away from the centrality of the proclamation of **Christ crucified**.

This will be a focus of the final chapter.

Suggestions for further reading

Banks, Robert, 1980. *Paul's Idea of Community: the early house churches in their historical setting*, Exeter, Paternoster Press, pp. 131–51

Karris, Robert J., 1993. 'The Pastoral Letters', in B.M. Metzger *et al.* (eds.), *The Oxford Companion to the Bible*, Oxford, OUP, pp. 573–6

Martin, Dale, 1990. *Slavery as Salvation: the metaphor of slavery in Pauline Christianity*, New Haven, YUP

Meeks, Wayne, 1983. *The First Urban Christians*, New Haven, YUP, p. 76

In this chapter, reference was also made to the following works

Combes, I.A.H., 1998. The Metaphor of Slavery in the Writings of the Early Church, Sheffield, JSNT Supplement Series

Crouch, J.E., 1972. *The Origin and Intention of the Colossian Haustafel*, Göttingen

Fiorenza, E. Schüssler, 1983. *In Memory of Her: a feminist theological reconstruction of Christian origins*, London, SCM

Lohse, Eduard, 1971. *Colossians and Philemon*, Philadelphia

Reading 1 Corinthians: 'Judge for yourselves'

At the end of each chapter there has been a section headed 'Reflecting on the message and the method'. This final short chapter attempts to do something similar for the whole of our study.

As he does in all his letters

The earliest surviving Christian writings we have are Paul's letters, written in the late 40s to the early 60s of the first century CE. Most or all of Paul's letters really did start out as letters, written at a distance from the churches they were sent to, and directed to individuals and the gathered community of Christians in that place. How far Paul expected them to be copied and passed on to other churches in other places is not always clear. Some of them are evidently particular to the concerns of one group of people – they are 'occasional' in the sense of being a response to one particular occasion or set of circumstances.

Very early on in the history of the Church, Paul's letters were known more widely than by the individual person or church to which any one letter was addressed. The author of 2 Peter (perhaps writing 110–20 CE) refers to what Paul wrote, saying that he speaks about the end of the world 'as he does in all his letters' (2 Pet. 3:16). This suggests a widespread use of a *body* of Paul's letters fifty or so years after his death, and seems to indicate a perception of his ministry in the Church as being of widespread or universal significance. (It may or may not comfort you to know that the author of 2 Peter did not find Paul easy reading. He says in the same verse, 'There are some things in them hard to understand . . .')

Paul's letters have been tremendously influential in the formation and the development of all forms of Christianity from the first century to the twenty-first. Many people make the claim that Paul is rightly considered the *founder* of Christianity – not disputing that the *foundation* is Jesus Christ – crediting Paul with articulating and shaping, as preacher and pastor, the beliefs that followed Christ's death and resurrection.

We preach Christ crucified

It has been possible to trace in 1 Corinthians a theology of subordination, patterned on Christ crucified and under the Lordship of Christ. In church order Paul assumes a 'dialectical authority' of mutual service and urges the community similarly to use gifts of the one Spirit of God, submissively for the edification of all the members. Within this pattern, in divisions reflecting different socioeconomic status, Paul expects the more powerful to submit to those who, outside the church, are their social subordinates. Women are free from at least some of the constraints of patriarchal-style marriage and, with certain socially ordained conditions, free to exercise leadership and ministry in the community. In each area of order, subjection to Christ and to God is paramount.

Neither this acceptance of the sovereignty of Christ, nor submission to each other, is a matter of command for the first readers, but both are essentially voluntary (like Christ's to God, 1 Cor. 15:28), and in the case of fellow Christians it is a mutual submission. Paul's own authority derives from the same source and follows the same pattern, of service and imitation of Christ crucified.

Love-patriarchy

Some analyses of these aspects of Paul's teaching describe his ethics as reflecting an ethos that Theissen has called 'love-patriarchalism'.

> This love-patriarchalism takes social differences for granted but ameliorates them through an obligation of respect and love, an obligation imposed on those who are socially stronger. From the weaker are required subordination, fidelity and esteem. (1982, p. 107)

Troeltsch, some decades before and without using this term, describes such an ethos as follows:

This is the type of Christian patriarchalism founded upon the religious recognition of and the religious overcoming of earthly inequality. There was a certain preparation for this in late Judaism, but it receives its special colour from the warmth of the Christian idea of love, through the inclusion of all in the Body of Christ . . . Its basic idea [is] of the willing acceptance of given inequalities, and of making them fruitful for the ethical values of personal relationships . . . All action is the service of God and is a responsible office, authority as well as obedience. As stewards of God the great must care for the small, and as servants of God the little ones must submit to those who bear authority; and since in doing so both meet in the service of God, inner religious equality is affirmed. (1931, p. 78)

This describes a type of New Testament ethics – and one which some Christians today would subscribe to – though, importantly, it lacks an eschatological perspective, and seems not to draw on a theology of **Christ crucified**. The ethics of the Pastorals, and of the Household Codes of Colossians and Ephesians could be described as love-patriarchalist. There wives, children and slaves are exhorted to be subject or obey; husbands, fathers and masters are exhorted to love, not to provoke and to treat justly. The differences of power remain unchallenged but the obligation of those with more power is to treat subordinates gently.

The term is not particularly discussed in contemporary scholarship on Paul (after the usual flurry of scholarly approval, disapproval and qualification following Theissen's publications). The phenomenon it describes, however, is prevalent – both in the assumptions and conclusions of some biblical scholarship and in some Christian communities today.

Be subject to one another

The work we have done in Philemon and 1 Corinthians in the chapters above challenges the idea that this ethos defines Paul's world-order and ethics. Theissen does find 'primitive Christian love-patriarchalism' in 1 Corinthians: 'We encounter [love-patriarchalism] particularly in the deutero-Pauline and pastoral letters but it is already evident in Paul (namely in 1 Cor 7:21ff.; 11:3–16)', (1982,

p. 107). Is he right? This sort of analysis certainly acknowledges Paul's 'quietist' tendencies (e.g. 1 Cor. 10:32, **Give no offence to Jews or to Greeks or to the church of God**), his practical compromises (e.g. 11:34, **If you are hungry, eat at home**) and his preparedness to limit and qualify the eschatological freedoms of a socially subordinate group (e.g. 14:34–5, **women should be silent in the churches . . . If there is anything they desire to know, let them ask their husbands at home**).

However, we have also seen that the voluntarily self-subordinating love of Paul's teaching in 1 Corinthians is not the paternalism that keeps a **weaker** or more vulnerable person subordinate by its tolerance of inferiority. Love-patriarchalism promotes the acceptance of inequalities, even if they are 'ameliorated' by respect or love. Paul, however, does not accept that a fellow believer is not to be given equal status – as a brother or sister **for whom Christ died** (1 Cor. 8:11) – even if they are **weak**. To be weak in this ethos is not to be 'less' but to be 'vulnerable' and therefore to have, in a way, a *greater* claim.

Paul's strategy therefore is not to accept a 'given inequality' but to reduce the gap between the two different positions to nothing. So Paul becomes **weak . . . to win the weak** (9:22). He writes with authority, but it is a 'dialectical authority' (Holmberg 1980, p. 186) diffusing that authority into the local churches. The rich are to refrain from private suppers so as to express that there is no inequality in Christ in the eschatological fellowship of love. The female prophets are 'covered' not to indicate subservience to their husbands but to manifest their own authority under Christ. These things do not indicate acceptance of inequalities but a reversal of social hierarchies.

Dale Martin (describing the ethos in question as 'benevolent patriarchalism', 1990, p. 128) characterises it as the view of the 'strong' in Corinth (1 Cor. 8), whom Paul corrects with his presentation of himself as **a slave** (9:19) and even **the rubbish of the world** (4:13), rather than their model of benevolent but superior leader.

Ironically, if the love-patriarchalists were right, none of the issues in 1 Corinthians need have been raised at all. The problems and conflicts would not have arisen if Paul's gospel had not called into the community, on an equal footing, people of sharply differentiated social status who believed in the call to members of one Body, having **the same care for one another** (1 Cor. 12:25).

I would not, however, deny that the 'benevolent patriarchalism' of the Household Codes and even (frankly) the misogyny of the Pastorals might not lead back in part to some of Paul's compromises and conditions, his partial conformity to old-order patriarchy in questions concerning married relations.

Love . . . does not insist on its own way

What of ourselves as new readers of these letters – do we have the same freedom as those first readers to judge for ourselves? Paul's letters, written to particular people about the issues of their lives, are now part of the canon of Christian Scriptures, and yet his letters remain texts whose meaning and significance is disputed. When the authority accorded to 'Scripture' is discussed, Paul's letters furnish several examples where radically different positions are taken as to how far what he has written should be normative for Christian belief and practice. It was Paul himself who wrote that Christianity is a religion of the spirit rather than the letter (see 2 Cor. 3:6), so it is right and good that there is a subjective, experiential element in the response of a reader of Paul just as there was in the writer (cf. Hammer 1993, p. 67).

If we apply the ethos of love-patriarchalism to Paul's writing of the letter and to our reading of it, we are in an unequal relationship with him: he has 'authority' and we need to have 'obedience'. This is not how Paul thinks he is addressing his reader, but he writes to Philemon saying, **If you consider me your partner** . . . (Philem. 17).

What makes a Christian response (a response in accord with Paul's own gospel) to reading what Paul has written? Is it to do what Paul *says* or to do what Paul *does*? If we do merely what he says, we read his teaching on behaviour in public worship and hold that it is necessary for women to wear a hat to church (whatever the culture of hats and bare heads around us). If we do what he does, we apply the principles of his theology to our situation as he did to his, and judge for ourselves what will build up the community, exercise God-given authority and gifts, and give no unnecessary offence to those within or without.

Shaw even suggests that 'we can only learn from Paul if we submit his writing to the criticism which he himself invites. To elevate his texts by ascribing to them an infallible authority is to condemn the church to repeat indefinitely his mistakes' (1983, p. 184).

In the ethos of 'love-patriarchalism', love ameliorates the situation of those with unequal power. Paul believed in a love that was transformative – the transforming power of the death and resurrection of Jesus, which was *effective* in the life of Christian communities, and effective in church order, social patterns and domestic relations. Paul does expect, in practical situations, the Christians of Corinth to live in Christ, the power of God and the wisdom of God, and to do so by voluntary subordination, in the **foolishness** of Christ crucified.

For Paul, the wisdom and power of systems of social stratification are to be brought to nothing – **For God's foolishness is wiser than human wisdom, and God's weakness is stronger than human strength** (1:25). Paul empowers his readers to know this and to respond, to Christ and to each other.

Reflecting on the message and the method

This was an exercise suggested at the end of Chapter 2:

> 'You have now read the whole letter, and some parts of it in more detail. Record now a summary of what you think the letter is about, what Paul's relationship is like with his correspondents, and what you think are key ideas in Paul's theology. You will then have a record to return to at the end of this study and will be able to see how far you have revised or confirmed your initial opinion.'

✎   What are now your conclusions about Paul's message, and about his method?

Suggestions for further reading

Elliott, Neil, 1994. *Liberating Paul: the justice of God and the politics of the apostle*, Sheffield, SAP

Evans, Robert, 1999. *Using the Bible: Studying the Text*, London, Darton, Longman and Todd

Goldingay, John, 1987. *Models of Scripture*, Carlisle, Paternoster Press

Hammer, Raymond, 'Authority of the Bible', in B.M. Metzger *et al.* (eds.), 1993. *The Oxford Companion to the Bible*, Oxford, OUP, pp. 65–8

Savage, Timothy B., 1996. *Power through Weakness: Paul's understanding of the Christian ministry in 2 Corinthians*, SNTP 86, Cambridge, CUP

Strange, William, 2000. *Authority of the Bible*, London, Darton, Longman and Todd

In this chapter, reference was also made to the following works

Holmberg, B., 1978. *Paul and Power: the structure of authority in the primitive church as reflected in the Pauline epistles*, Uppsala, CWK Gleerup

Martin, Dale, 1990. *Slavery as Salvation: the metaphor of slavery in Pauline Christianity*, New Haven, YUP

Shaw, G., 1983. *The Cost of Authority: manipulation and freedom in the New Testament*, London, SCM

Theissen, Gerd, 1982. *The Social Setting of Pauline Christianity*, Edinburgh, T&T Clark

Troeltsch, Ernst, 1931. *The Social Teaching of the Christian Churches,* 2 vols., London

Index